My Lemonade Life

A memoir of living with love, laughter and
now . . . cancer

Also by Paul S. Bodner

The Lemonade Series

A Daddy's World

Teaching with Love, Laughter & Lemonade

Living with Love, Laughter & Lemonade

My Lemonade Life

A memoir of living with love, laughter and now . . . cancer

Paul S. Bodner

Strategic Consulting, LLC

ISBN 978-0-9904159-0-9
ISBN 978-0-9904159-1-6

Published in the United States of America by
Strategic Consulting, LLC, 4596 Bersaglio St.,
Las Vegas, NV 89135
www.paulbodner.com

Cover photograph: Mike Stotts
Cover and book design/format: Jason A. Martin

Printed in the United States of America by
CREATESPACE, an Amazon.com company

First Edition

Dedicated to my wife, my best friend and my soul mate, Ellen, who still makes me laugh. And to our grandchildren, who can perhaps learn from my life lessons and create a future for themselves filled with more love, laughter, and lemonade: Talia, Elie and Orly Bodner; Noah and Ethan Bodner; Jessica and Alex Nathan; Jake Blaney and Jack Millstein.

CONTENTS

ACT TWO
Oy, There Are New Lemons

Living a life that matters is all I ever wanted. I never thought of it being over someday—instead, I always wondered what would be next. That led to a life of reflection and, later, a focused sense of appreciation.

Nothing is forever, and no one gets out of this game alive. By accepting these truths and letting go of trying to control death, I'm now more fully engaged in life.

But the clock is ticking. On March 12, 2012, I was diagnosed with stage 4 lung cancer—so the time for me to tell "what really happened" is now. The odds of my being around for more than a few years are not good. My attitude is forever, but my prognosis suggests I get it done today.

Thus, this book. I'm not a movie star, a world-renowned artist or a household name. I'm just a guy who tried to keep things interesting. Occasionally, I did have an adventure that went from the ordinary to the extraordinary. Lessons were learned along the way—stories filled with love, laughter, and lemonade.

This book shares those stories of what really happened with my life's lemons—pits and all. My hope is that they will help shine a light on your everyday life, transforming it with a purpose and a lemonade attitude.

There is no such thing as coincidence. Everything happens for a reason. Sometimes you have to work, think or pray very hard at finding that reason—but I promise you, it all makes sense.

It had been a difficult week. Just five days earlier, I was carefree. My life felt like it was in perfect balance—but on March 12, 2012, things were about to change.

The previous Sunday, I had been playing golf and noticed hip pain that progressively grew worse. I went to see my physician friend—Dr. David Silverberg—the same doc who performed my wife Ellen's hip replacement surgery a year earlier. Yeah, I know. Hips, bones, lungs. We sound like we were a mess. But actually, we ate right, worked out, looked good, felt good and were good people. Yet, like any hard-working machine, sometimes the parts need fixing.

My doc did some tests and didn't like what he saw. So yep, more tests. After a few days and a million pokes later, he ordered a biopsy of my left hip—and again didn't like what he saw.

Now eventually I figured this out: When a doctor "doesn't like what he sees," it's like hearing a joke that starts out with, "There's good news and bad news—which do you want to hear first?"

And so we waited patiently for the pathology report. Not! Please, I even hate waiting for water to boil. So by the next day, I was going nuts.

WHEN YOU'RE OVER 65 AND THE PHONE RINGS AFTER 10 PM, IT CAN'T BE GOOD

That evening, my wife and I were in our comfortable chairs, watching TV. Then, the phone rang.

"Hello," I said, hoping that it was either a wrong number or a knuckle-head from a political poll calling to disturb our evening.

"Hi, Paul, this is David Silverberg."

It took a minute to process, primarily because I was so focused on the call being from someone—anyone—other than him.

"Hi, David. I normally would say, 'good to hear from you' . . . but at this hour, I'm not so sure. What's up?"

"I just got off the phone with the pathologist, confirming the biopsy, so I wanted to call you myself."

The wheels in my head were spinning. I did everything I could to stay calm. I watched as Ellen turned off the TV with the remote, sat straight up and motioned for me to put him on speaker.

"Okay," I said, "tell me what's going on."

I let him know my wife was also listening in case he wanted to "make nice" with his words. Fortunately, my doctor friend was thoughtful and—as nice as he was—spoke the truth to me.

"The report shows some abnormal cell growth in the hip area, which has been identified. It's adenocarcinoma."

The news was hard for me to understand. It was the worst possible news . . . or so I thought. It was difficult for me to breathe, but I asked him to go on.

"Adenocarcinoma is lung cancer—a non-smoker's lung cancer. It's common and can be treated. Do you understand?"

I heard the words and certainly understood what he just said, but I could not—would not—accept them as accurate! I mean, lung cancer?

"David, my pain was in my hip—the biopsy you did was on my hip, right?"

Dr. Silverberg knew my sense of humor and didn't take the bait.

"Yes, that's right. The cancer in your lungs metastasized to your hip, but it came from your lungs, where there are small nodules."

"How many small nodules?"

"They're scattered, 5mm or less in size—looks like there are about 15 of them."

Again, silence. All I saw were the eyes of my wife, the love of my life, the supporter of my dreams. Her eyes were moist with concern and very red.

"Paul, I've talked to Ron Klein. He's standing by to take your call. He'll make sure you see the right oncologist as soon as possible—and I'm here 24/7. I know you will have questions, so call me tomorrow and we can talk some more."

Dr. Ron Klein was another great friend—a pediatric oncologist, truly an angelic spirit known to everyone as a great doc.

I got off the phone with David and turned to Ellen. We've been together for 16 years (second marriage for us both). Between us, we have five kids and nine grandchildren, but have known each other since we were 14. Growing up in Teaneck, New Jersey, we were best friends—but more on that later.

Ellen was the first to speak. "Well, now we know."

"Yep, now we know."

The truth is, we both had been thinking it was cancer. When the doc had said those famous words after the biopsy—"not crazy about what I saw in there"—we knew my pain wasn't going to just be a groin pull.

But then our lemons-to-lemonade positive thinking kicked in.

"He did say it was pretty common and that we can treat it," I said to my wife.

"Absolutely! And, actually, thank God it's lung cancer and not melanoma!"

We looked at each other and started to laugh. I understood exactly what she meant. Back in 1999, while we were swimming at my daughter-in-law Ronit's family lake house, her sister Riki—a recent medical school graduate at the time—noticed a beauty mark on my hip. And, yes, she also "didn't like what she saw."

Good thing. I found out it was stage 1 melanoma and had it removed, never to be heard from since.

"We'll figure this out together and beat this thing. I know we will," Ellen said.

"I know, I know. And I believe that, too, but I just don't get it. Lung cancer. Where in the world did this come from—and why?"

It was all quite confusing, but I knew it would have to wait until morning.

WHEN LEMONS POUR DOWN—GET YOUR UMBRELLA OUT AND START MAKING LEMONADE

By 6 am, I was out of bed. I had a cup of coffee and started making a list.

1. Call Dr. Klein for info.
2. Call back Dr. Silverberg for follow up.
3. Google "adenocarcinoma."
4. Call my sister, Sue.
5. Call my kids.

Ellen walked into the kitchen, got some coffee and gave me a sweet smile. "How are you doing?"

"I need more information—I started writing a list."

"You wrote a list?"

"Well, yeah. I've been up all night and didn't want to forget something!"

"Did you remember everything?"

"Not really. But I can't remember what I forgot, so I guess it'll come back to me."

In our family, I'm the list maker. Ellen is the bridge crosser, going through life without worrying about stuff "until you cross that bridge." Interestingly, our diverse approaches have worked well in our marriage over the years.

So here we were . . . at another bridge.

"I think we need to get a second opinion—on everything," I said.

Ellen quickly agreed and thought for a minute. "We have access to other medical opinions within our family and friends. We even have some friends who have friends who might be able to guide us."

"Good idea."

The next few hours flew by. We made all the calls on my list. I reached Dr. Ron Klein, who immediately referred me to Dr. Jim Sanchez, a prominent oncologist and head of his practice, The Comprehensive Cancer Centers.

That connection was to become a big deal. We got lucky. I could smell the sweet aroma of lemonade already.

Mike and Andrea Leven, our relatively new friends at the time, stepped up and became family. They immediately made a call that allowed me to be accepted as a patient at MD Anderson, an internationally recognized cancer hospital and research center in Houston. By mid-morning, I was scheduled to be on a plane in a few days, seeing one of their docs for an opinion.

We believe Mike and Andrea were placed here by God to help us. They had moved to Las Vegas from Atlanta "strictly" because of his job—but I think their move was one of those God winks to help me as well.

Then it was time for us to make some tough calls—the hardest ones were to our kids: my boys and their wives. Needless to say, my son Zack and his wife, Ronit, along with my son Gabe and his wife, Tamara, were quite concerned. They made immediate arrangements to come out for a visit. My wife's kids (Wendy, Adam and Jason) have been in my life long enough that they, too, reached out with love and support.

BREWING LEMONS

Soon after I finished all those phone calls, I had a very surreal experience. Just a few days before, I hadn't considered how much time I had left in the "life bottle." That changed. I quickly realized that I'm facing a limited supply.

I'm not talking about some morbid sense of doom. Nope, instead that realization produced within me a calming focus on finding truth . . . a truth that was about to become the basis of how I live.

It gave me clarity. I now saw death as a part of life. Sure, some things are out of my—and your—control. And yet—not wanting to sound all Mary Poppins-ish—when the biggest lemon of life is staring you right in the face, you and I can do something, something proactive that will change our lives. Know what it is? Let go of the control buttons! Instead, trust in whatever spiritual sources of inspiration you have in your life . . . and use them.

I've long been a spiritual person who strongly believes in God granting me a life of purpose, which I share at more length in this book. But we all need to find whatever source inspires us to have hope and stay focused with that attitude, no matter how hard it is to take that lemon and make sweet lemonade. If I can do it, you can, too. Really.

Here's what I did. I grabbed a pen and made another list, calling it "Old Lemons." I started to think back to my earliest life lemons and how they became lemonade. But most importantly, I tried to discover the reasons why things happened to me and what I could do about them.

The exercise helped—and led to my writing down my most memorable lemons-to-lemonade moments. My hope is that they will make you laugh, reflect and get a whole new perspective on your own lemon challenges.

ACT ONE

Ah, Those Old Lemons

ONE

Teaneck Times

Old friends are the best friends because you know each other's history. That way, you're always able to be honest with each other because you both know the truth.

All my dreams began in Teaneck, New Jersey. No kidding.

It was a balmy Jersey night back in 1956. My family, like millions of others, was gathered—as always—around the TV. The highlight of our week was about to begin: *The Milton Berle Show.*

Typical of most post-WWII Americans, my folks worked hard with little downtime for laughter or rest. Mr. Television (aka "Uncle Miltie") gave them a break . . . one that would transform their week with his gags, improv skits, pie-in-the-face routines and, most of all, his outlandish cross-dressing act.

That hour of laughter was the start of it all for me—it was where fun and the dream of fun were born. The workweek may have had its share of lemons for my parents, but I watched firsthand how humor turned it into sweet lemonade. There was one thing I knew for sure. I wanted more of it—lots more.

And that's when I got the bright idea to mimic Milton Berle to get my dad—whose name just happened to be Milton and who was known as "Uncle Miltie" in the family—to laugh even harder. It just seemed a natural move.

One night, at the top of the *The Milton Berle Show* hour, I came prancing down the stairs wearing my sister's dress and yelling, "Make up!" That was the moment on the show when Uncle Miltie would get the pie and the biggest laugh, especially from my folks. But in this case, my family looked at me as if I had lost my mind.

Within seconds, my sister screamed in a demanding tone, "Put your pants on, Paul, and take off my crinoline dress!"

Meanwhile, my mother was taking a Brownie photograph. And my dad? Well, he was clutching his chest. I didn't know if he was sick from laughing or crying.

But I accomplished my goal—I made them laugh. That fun bit became a legend in the family for many years to come. And it also formed my lifetime interest in making as many lemons into lemonade as possible. It also was the moment I realized that as hard as life can be, there is always a way to make it feel better—through love, laughter, and making lemonade out of lemons.

LIFE IN THE SWAMP

We lived in a brand new house on Sandra Place that would have been fine—if it weren't for the fact that the backyard had just been filled in with dirt because the *yard* used to be a swamp.

But it all worked for me. I was one of the original swamp people, having loads of fun digging for treasures, like beer cans and cigarette lighters. I even remember a tractor sinking out of sight in our backyard. They had to bring another tractor to haul it out. Now that was great stuff to watch.

My dad worked with a friend of his in a shoe store in Hackensack called Kates Brothers. They sold shoes for people with bad feet, specializing in children's shoes. I had flat feet, so that was a good thing. I remember going into the store and watching my dad put the arch supports in my shoes—even in my sneakers. They felt really uncomfortable, but he said it would help. Mmm, not sure about that one. My feet are still flat!

My mom was a homemaker and had a part-time bookkeeper job. I never heard my parents discuss money, but I knew my mom would come home and save a little in a jar in the kitchen. She called it a *pushkie*.

A day didn't go buy when she wouldn't buy us ice cream with that money. So when the Good Humor Man would come around, there was mom with just enough money to buy us whatever we wanted.

My sister Sue & her husband Bernie, who have shared a lifetime of lemonade with me.

My sister Sue was fun to be around—most of the time. Sure, we had our share of sibling fighting, but I was her little brother and she protected me. She even taught me how to dance. Every day after school, Sue's friends would come over to our house to watch *American Bandstand* on TV. I was the only boy . . . lucky me, right? But that "old lemon" of an experience turned into some pretty sweet lemonade because I actually became a pretty good dancer, thanks to Sue and her friends.

Life was good in Teaneck for a Jewish boy like me—one who loved to read, write, play ball and hang out with friends. In fact, many of my elementary school friendships I still have today.

EISENHOWER STORY

Two of my best friends—Elliot Sainer and David Hinden—came from Longfellow Elementary School. We met when I was being introduced as a new fourth grade student, fresh from Washington, DC. My teacher, Miss Bianchi, was the most beautiful and caring woman I had ever seen. And she liked me!

So when Miss Bianchi asked me to tell the class a little about my days living in the nation's capitol, I proceeded to tell the story that is now legendary in our family.

"Well, when my family and I lived in Washington, we lived close to the White House. We loved President Eisenhower so much that we celebrated when he was elected—and even went to his inaugural parade. We stood with the rest of the huge crowd gathered along the streets of Pennsylvania Ave. But when the president's car passed by, I waved with both hands and fell off my bicycle!"

A hush fell across the classroom . . . along with a look of disbelief on my teacher's face. But she didn't stop me, so I kept on weaving my lemonade story.

"When President Eisenhower saw me fall off my bike, he stopped the procession and directed the Secret Service to come to my rescue. Next thing I knew, a Secret Service man who looked as tall as the Washington Monument asked me if I was all right. I was so amazed that all I could do was nod that I was okay. He placed my broken bike into the trunk of the Secret Service's car—and I got to ride along! He said he would drop me off at a point where my parents could pick me up. Riding in that car in the procession was a blast! And so, that's why my family always voted for President Eisenhower."

There's no doubt my rendition of Eisenhower's inaugural parade set the tone for my continued popularity at Longfellow Elementary.

It also has been a story whose accuracy has been questioned through the years, particularly from my two friends, Elliot and David. In fact, a few years ago, they prepared a birthday present for me—a headline from the *Washington Post* that read, "Eisenhower Refutes Boy on Bike Story!"

But it's my story, and I'm sticking to it.

WASHINGTON, THE BACKSTORY

Okay, so here's what really went on in DC. For eight years, my family lived on a tree-lined street just a few miles from the White House. My mom, Ruth, fondly described our home as an "early brownstone," but I learned later it was actually a post-WWII, red-brick attached house.

Bodner celebration with grandma & grandpa up front—but who is the bride in the far left? No one knows.

Come to think of it, my mom was a great example of how to live a lemonade life. She had rheumatic fever as a child that left her with heart disease. And yet, three heart valve replacements later, nothing stopped her from enjoying life. At every bar mitzvah, she would be out on the floor dancing to the *hora*.

My dad had ambitions to become an accountant. But when World War II reared its head, he left college to serve in the army and later worked in a shoe store in DC. Visiting him was like going to a playground because of the huge x-ray machine that was smack in the middle of the store.

I'd put my feet under the screen and *snap!*—a photo would come out showing my bony toes and just how much I had grown. Of course, back then, we had no idea that the radiation in the machine was probably using a million zaps.

I took photos of my feet for hours. My dad didn't care; he was happy that I was busy. Then one day, he came into my bedroom and saw all my feet photos hanging on the wall. He bent over and just laughed and laughed. There were very few times I remember my dad laughing so hard his face hurt, but this was one of them.

My mother's family also lived in the DC area, so they were very much in our lives. My grandparents had emigrated from Russia with the wave of Jewish people in the early 1900s. They only spoke Yiddish and some broken English.

"Listen, my little one, ven I smile, and pinch your cheeks and say *Shana Punim*—dats a good thing! So don't complain!"

That's when I learned the art of communication had nothing to do with what language you were speaking. When my grandparents wanted me to listen, all it took was a finger in the air. When they wanted me to eat, borscht was put in front of me and a chair was pulled out. And when they entertained me with stories "from the old country," I was mystified. Even though the stories were in Yiddish or broken English and I couldn't understand a thing they said, I hung onto every word.

My grandfather chained-smoked Lucky Strike cigarettes. They were non-filter, and the tobacco wouldn't just go up in smoke—it also would stick to his tongue. My grandfather would focus on spitting it out . . . or spitting it on whomever was nearby, which was usually me.

But I got smart. I learned to watch his mouth. His tongue would curl just before that *ptoy* moment. Out it came. I would bob and weave to dodge the bullet, but occasionally he would get me. Actually, I think he knew what I was doing and enjoyed the sport.

My grandpa was a political man—perhaps the result of leaving Europe where his family was treated badly. In the US, he could live his life in a country granting freedom of religion. Nothing would ever again be taken for granted.

It wasn't unusual for one of our family dinner table conversations to end with raised voices and strained veins—and always with a finger wagging high in the air, "Kindelach! America is a vunderful ting!"

My grandpa's stories of being saved at Ellis Island by Jewish people wearing blue hats—the identifiable sign of a member of the Hebrew Immigration Aid Society—really impacted my entire life. He reminded me about our human responsibility and how life can be made remarkable by the kindness of total strangers. It taught me that *tzedakah* (charity) is everyone's responsibility. That's why I believe we should always give what we can, knowing there is always someone who needs it more than we do—a penny, a nickel or a dollar. Just give something.

FLIPPIN' THE BIRD

When I was in second grade, my parents announced that we were leaving DC and moving to New Jersey. We spent a rather unmemorable two years living in a garden apartment in East Paterson before later settling down in Teaneck.

Well, almost unmemorable.

Our neighbor, Urban Svaard, was from Sweden. His accent and mannerisms made me laugh. But when we had an argument, Urban would hold up his middle finger in the air. Confused on what it meant, I asked him.

"It means I'm mad at you!"

So the next day, when my dad came home from work and yelled at me for not taking the dog for a walk, I got really mad at him . . . and gave him "the bird."

Out came the belt. Whack!

"But Urban told me," I wailed.

"Urban told you what?"

"Urban said shooting the bird meant I was mad at you!"

"What? Maybe in Iceland or wherever the hell he's from, but where we live, it's bad and dirty—and you'll never do that again. Hear me?"

Now, that was a really big lemonade lesson learned.

CYNTHIA'S KISS

Teaneck was a fast-growing town. They soon built a new school closer to my home called Hawthorne Elementary.

I was 12 years old, in the fifth grade, and my genes were kicking in. My neighbor, Cynthia Schwartz, was in my same grade, so we became school-mates. We also were in Hebrew school together, so we would walk and talk a lot. I'd walk to her house, then we would take a wooded path at the end of our street to save about three blocks on our way to school.

Our parents told us there were bad kids hanging out in that path, so we should be careful. I kept a look out, but never saw any of them—until one day. The bad kids showed up, carrying knives and wearing hip-high boots. They started to say some pretty gross things and make some stupid comments.

"Hey, kid! Do you know what this is?" A tall, gangly, pimple-faced teen held up what looked like a dead animal.

"No, and I don't care," I bravely stood my ground.

"These are muskrat skins, and we sell them for 25 cents each—you want in?"

Cynthia peered behind my shoulder for a closer look. They were muddy, rat-like rodents, draped over the shoulders of 15-year-old kids, who I imagined were killers.

"You can go with us Saturday. We'll give you a nickel for every skin you snare. Now, you in?"

With Cynthia clutching my jacket sleeve, I agreed to meet them—as long as they would never bother us again. They laughed, and we made a time to meet.

As we left the pathway and continued walking home, Cynthia was shivering with fear. I made a gallant move and put my arm around her. It was the first time I had ever attempted such a romantic gesture—and it felt great. Cynthia came closer to me, and my hand slid down her arm to find an open, willing hand to hold. We stayed like that through the rest of the walk home.

She became my first girlfriend, and we walked together every day. But I learned quickly that holding hands wouldn't last. When we were in sight of any potential neighbors—or worse yet, our friends—we dropped hands. We never talked about it, but we both knew it was best to keep it that way.

One day, we were sitting on a stretch of grassy lawn and talking. We held hands . . . and then it happened. She agreed to see how long we could kiss without taking a breath! It was miraculous. We locked lips, mentally counting until we couldn't hold out any longer. Panting with exhaustion, we finally got to a full 60 seconds. It was a first kiss that couldn't have been sweeter.

BIZARRO WORLD OF WILLIAM TELL

Cynthia was a special friend in many ways—my first kiss, first girlfriend and the one who would introduce me to theatre. She played the flute in the band and encouraged me to take up the trumpet, which I did, but badly. That was okay because it led me to the arts and hanging around creative kids, like my friend, Barry Frank.

Barry was cast in a play, *William Tell*, so he encouraged me to try out. With Cynthia's support, I auditioned and got the part of William Tell.

We rehearsed our lines, had costumes for our parts and prepared for the big night—a one-night-only performance for a PTA meeting.

Playing the famed William Tell meant my "shooting" an apple off the head of my brave son, performed by Barry. We were ready for the bright lights of Broadway . . . but things didn't work out quite as planned.

Just at the moment of drawing my bow back, the lights were to crackle. In the dark, the apple on Barry's head would be exchanged for an apple with an arrow in it. However, when the lights came up, the apple was indeed exchanged for one with an arrow through it—but the arrow was pointing directly at me!

Well, the audience was hysterical, applauding wildly. Barry and I took our bows. It was my first theatrical taste of laughter and it was addictive. That was it. I was hooked on acting.

Looking back on that event, I also had begun the journey of turning dreams of who I wanted to be, into the person I would eventually become. Call it the *Lemonade Theory* or *Pleasure-Pain Principle*, but I learned that when you go deep inside to register your feelings and identify those great influencers in your life, good things are born.

My first romance with Cynthia, my introduction to theatre, my love of the stage, and my planting seeds as a storyteller. They were all about turning embarrassing and challenging moments into laughter. That was the beginning of making lemonade dreams out of many, funny lemons!

TWO

The Art of Becoming Very Jewish

*Act as if someone you respect is watching—even when they aren't,
you'll be doing the right thing.*

Living a Jewish life can be a bit confusing—especially when I was growing up. Sure, my parents followed the typical Jewish customs, like going to synagogue pretty often and celebrating all our religious holidays. The Jewish Federation logo was our bumper sticker. But when it came to being kosher, my parents shook things up a bit. They believed their kosher obligation only applied to what we ate in the house, not what our bodies consumed anywhere else.

So every year on one of our most important holidays, Passover, we did what all good Jews would do: go crazy for a whole week ridding the house of any *chametz*—any food made of fermented grain. We switched the dishes, silverware, pots and pans, then cleaned the whole house from top to bottom.

So far, so good . . . until we would go out to eat. Invariably, we would head over to our favorite Chinese place and order our favorite dish—shrimp in lobster sauce! Totally *not* kosher.

Yep, it was a strange Bodner tradition. But, as the saying goes, "It wasn't right or wrong, it was just their way!"

HOLD THE BALONEY

My friends didn't escape the Bodner-kosher conundrum either. Normally, if my pals Ray and Gary came over to my house after school, we would play some basketball, stickball, or curb ball—games that required little equipment and little money—and work hard to be the best in the neighborhood. Then, after we played, we would head into my house for a snack. But there was this one day . . .

Ray and Gary usually liked the way my mom would make a peanut butter and jelly sandwich—fresh Wonder® Bread with Welch's® grape jelly and Skippy® Creamy Peanut Butter. And, of course, just enough of each. Then she would cut the sandwich in quarters. It was really delicious.

However, one time when my mom wasn't home, we went into the kitchen with the intent of having some milk and cookies. But Gary found the bologna, made himself a sandwich, and sat down with a glass of milk. *Oy!* My mom arrived a few minutes later and took one look and actually screamed. She ran over to Gary, picked up his glass, plate and silverware, then ordered the three of us to follow her.

We were a bit scared, not knowing where she was going. I had never seen my mom act like that, so we just did what she asked. We followed her into the backyard, where she proceeded to hand us each a shovel.

"Start digging."

I knew she wasn't going to kill us—or hoped she wasn't. We obeyed until the hole was the depth she wanted.

"That's enough," she said, bending over and placing the glass, plate, knife and fork into the empty hole.

She stood up, walked back a step, covered her eyes, and said a prayer in Hebrew. I looked over at my friends. They didn't know what to do either. But, since they were also Jewish, they just covered their eyes. I'm pretty sure they also prayed—for what, I really don't know. Probably their lives!

Although my mom was very serious about the prayer, I also think she did that for an extra dramatic effect on us. Truth be told, I think she peeked at us through her fingers.

But I can tell you this much. I never mixed milk products with meat products in our home ever again—and neither did my friends. That little digging exercise taught me to respect the customs of being kosher (or kosher style).

TOUGH GUYS

Being Jewish meant going to Hebrew school—a time filled with strong memories, some very sweet and some very bitter. It was an expectation that from 10 to 13 years of age, we would attend Hebrew school and become a bar mitzvah. There was no discussion on the subject. That's the way it was. And you got nice presents when you had a bar mitzvah party, so it was all good.

My bar mitzvah was especially memorable because three of us shared the day. That's right . . . three of us. Teaneck was so Jewish, we had to double up—and then triple up—on *every* Saturday morning, sharing our bar mitzvah. In fact, mine was shared with a friend, who we'll call Larry B. Larry was a foot shorter than I was, so he needed a chair to stand on just to reach the microphone. Another bar mitzvah buddy, Ricky C., stuttered terribly. He was a great kid, but his stuttering added an extra hour to the service!

The Hebrew schoolteachers were the unsung heroes. How they actually paid their bills and made a living, I'll never know. But they made a difference. When I think of the little money they got, and the huge pain we were, I would like to see them all today and thank them—especially Mr. Seymour Herr (pronounced *hair*), our principal. He was as bald as a cue ball. You can only imagine the names we called him—and the grief we gave him: Mr. Herr, mmm . . . I'm so sorry.

Our Hebrew school was integrated as part of our Jewish Community Center, the Teaneck JCC. It definitely was the center of our lives. The building was the spiritual, cultural and physical center of all things—and the place you would find us as kids, hanging out and growing up. We learned a lot at the JCC, including that we had to know how to defend ourselves.

Here's what happened. We had a group of friends who were mostly Jewish. That meant that we, as Jews, couldn't get into the non-Jewish, toughest, most-likely-to-get-girls club for boys in town. There were two clubs: Ashaks and Vikings. Great names, and they looked great on their letter jackets. Very cool. So we called a meeting and decided the only thing we could do to compete with these guys was to form our own club: The ACES.

We went to our parents, got the money and ordered letter jackets with our club name—The ACES—emblazoned on the back of the jacket. However, we soon learned there was another club in the area (Paterson, NJ to be exact) that also was named The ACES. Double *oy*!

Well, the Paterson club didn't like the idea of our using their name. So they challenged us to a gang fight for the right to use the name. Now, we were a pretty smart group of kids, but not known for our fighting skills. Actually the one guy in the group who wasn't Jewish had Italian roots, so he was more than happy to be our bodyguard.

But a gang fight was out of the question. If we couldn't outfight them, we figured we could outthink them. My group of guys went into a survival meeting and came up with the solution. Since we already had ordered the letter jackets, but the name wasn't on them yet, all we had to do was make one change—spell the club name backward and add an "s." That's right, we became the SECAS.

We had a name no one else had—or wanted—and we would live to see another day. And we did. No other club has ever been named SECAS—ever.

BLACK EYE, SWOLLEN LIP & MY FRENCH HORN

If the other guy is a lot bigger and stronger, use your mind and you can usually outsmart them—*usually* being the operative word. But sometimes even being clever and using your mind isn't enough. So as part of my lemonade lessons, it would only be fair to say that standing up for what you believe and defending your values can sometimes require physical courage as well.

Case in point: When I was about 15 years old, I was leaving school, carrying my books and my French horn—yes, I played the French horn. I actually began in fifth grade playing the trumpet. But when I got to the school band, the teacher, Mr. Blanchard, said I had French horn lips, so I switched. It might have been because there were 18 trumpet players and only two French horn players . . . but I like to think it was because I had French horn lips.

So I was walking home one wintry day, and the tough guys in school starting bullying me around. I could usually talk my way out of things, but this time, I had had enough. They called me a *dirty Jew*, an expression that immediately makes you think of the Nazis. And every Jewish kid knows those stories. Needless to say, I was really angry.

I remember taking my heavy winter coat off, putting my books down, and then running at the bully full force. I can only tell you I screamed at him while I flailed away with my fists. I don't remember much, probably because he had me in a headlock. But I do remember he was even more surprised than I was that I fought back. Eventually, Mr. Nelson, the gym teacher, came to my rescue and stopped the fight.

The next day, I had a black eye and a swollen lip. My friends already had heard about my fighting the bully in school. So even though I was hurting, they made me feel great. And the bully? Suspended from school. His pals never bothered me again. Now that was one nasty lemon made into sweet lemonade.

Sometimes it's not about fighting, but about having the physical and mental courage to stand up for what you are and what you think is right.

THREE

Wild Afternoon with Marilyn

Take a position in life, and let it be known. You can always change your mind later—but take a position now. It will give you, and everyone around you, an honest picture of how you view things.

When puberty hits, there are girlfriends and then there are *girlfriends*. Ellen Levy was my childhood friend who was a girl—and who made it perfectly clear to anyone who asked that she was not my girlie-girlfriend. We both went out with the same group of friends, mostly from the Jewish community. She was the cutest one in the whole bunch, really. But I was the brother she never had, so I had other girlfriends . . . but not Ellen.

Our group of friends loved to go to the movies in Hackensack at the Fox or Oritani Theatre. Then we would go to Bischoff's on Cedar Lane to get ice cream sundaes. Sometimes we would go to the New England Pizza Shop for a near-beer to act like big shots. But it was innocent fun and none of us got into any trouble. Once though, I wandered from the usual crowd and learned a very important lesson.

It was a Saturday afternoon, and I had been at the record shop, probably looking for the latest Johnny Mathis record. I was a nut for his music. Sometimes my friend Larry and I would just browse through the bins filled with records. The store owner was so nice, allowing us to play them on his record player before we bought them.

On this memorable day, my friend didn't show, so I was alone . . . at least when I arrived.

"Hi, Paul. How are you?"

I glanced up and saw Marilyn, the really cute girl who hung out with the *other* guys—usually the members of the Ashaks or the Vikings. Our term for them? Hoods.

"Oh, hi, Marilyn. I'm fine—how are you doing?"

"I'm good! I was here looking for the new Johnny Mathis record and just found it. 'Chances Are' . . . it's sooooo great!"

I couldn't believe my ears. She not only loved Johnny Mathis, but she just bought his new record. That was very cool.

"Wow! I know—he's the best. I haven't heard the whole album, but I hear it's great."

Marilyn looked at me and just smiled.

"If you haven't heard it yet, why don't you come over to my house, and we can listen together. Okay?"

"Really? Wow! That would be great . . . but when?"

"You can come over now if you want."

I was stunned into silence. I knew this was a moment to be frozen in time—Marilyn asking me to listen to Johnny Mathis music.

"Absolutely! Let's go."

Marilyn told me to meet her at her house, which was just a few blocks away. I was on my bicycle—I was 15 and not driving yet—so I met her there within minutes. She was already at home and had the record player going. The sounds of Johnny Mathis filled the room.

Listening to Johnny Mathis music was like turning on the make-out switch. First you dance, then you smooch, and then you play around. And then, sometimes, you get surprised.

We had begun to do some smooching when the doorbell rang. A fellow high school student was at the door, working as a delivery boy for Miller's Drugstore, dropping off a prescription for Marilyn's mother. His name was Bobby Spinelli—one of the *other* guys. He saw me as she opened the door. I knew there was going to be a problem.

As soon as he left, I said my goodbyes to Marilyn, jumped on my bicycle and headed home. When I got in my house, my phone rang. It was my best friend, Larry.

"Paul, I just saw you speeding up Cedar Lane on your bicycle. I was with my parents in their car, did you see me?"

"No, I didn't see you."

"Well, where were you?"

And that was it. All he had to do was ask. I proceeded to tell him every-thing, down to the details, as all young boys do. Which meant I exaggerat-ed as well. Somewhere toward the end of my blabbing on and on about my sexy afternoon, I heard a voice on the extension.

"Oh, my God! That is the most disgusting thing I have ever heard!"

It was Paula, the girl of my dreams . . . sort of. She was a beautiful cheerleader. We all had a crush on Paula at one time or another. And she was Larry's neighbor, sitting at his house—he had set the whole thing up. Now, granted, he didn't know what I was going to say, but still. How em-barrassing!

By the next Monday, everyone knew about my wild afternoon with Marilyn, including her boyfriend, Tony Bucino. He marched into the high school cafeteria, stood over me with his big arms crossed like an Indian chief and made it perfectly clear that I should stay away from Marilyn—or else I'd have an unwanted nose job.

I nodded with absolute agreement, then watched as my friends had a mixture of fear and respect in their eyes—for me! To this day, David, a Yale attorney and one of my best friends who was there during my near-death experience, remembers it as one of the funniest moments in his high school career. He laughed so much the milk he was drinking came pouring out of his nose. Now *that* was funny.

I saw Marilyn later in school that day. We both knew what had hap-pened. I apologized first and hoped she didn't get into any trouble. She just smiled. I'll never forget what she said next.

"Hey, I couldn't care less about what Tony says. Let me know when you want to come by to finish listening to Johnny Mathis. I had fun!"

It was the nicest thing she could have said. It made me actually think about her for many, many years. I will always remember Marilyn as a very strong, very brave voice, who was not going to be told what she could or should do. She was very cool.

Big lesson learned there. Live your life the way you want, and let go of the people who are negative . . . especially if they're a member of the Ashaks or Vikings.

THE MAGIC OF DOO-WOP

*The original Stereos—I'm the fourth from the left. I **still** have those blue suede shoes.*

Teaneck was no Asbury Park, but we did have a passion for doo-wop music. And it was a sure thing to get the hottest cheerleaders interested in going out . . . so we formed a six-man rock 'n roll group: The Stereos. We actually wrote a few original songs, got to play at some Sweet 16 parties—we were definitely cheap to hire—and we actually became pretty good.

One day we found out about a talent contest at the Fox Theatre in

Hackensack, so we decided to enter. We rehearsed for several weeks, and the big day came. We had many of our friends there to stoke the audience meter—just like NBC's *Ted Mack and the Original Amateur Hour*—the louder the applause, the better chance we had of winning.

The thing is—we won! We actually did win the first prize, which turned out to be an opportunity to record a demo with a real New York producer. And so—he made arrangements to visit Teaneck and to meet with our parents, presenting them this *lifetime* opportunity.

He arrived at my friend Larry's home, where all our parents had gathered. The producer was wearing velvet pants, a pirate's shirt, and sporting a huge Elvis wave in front of his slicked-back hair. Our parents listened to him go on and on, then stopped him cold when he said his recording studio was in his New York apartment. Each parent got up, walked over and stood behind their kid.

Larry's parents: "He's going to be a doctor." (He became an attorney.)

Elliot's parents: "He's going to run a bank." (He became a successful hospital administrator and entrepreneur.)

Mark's parents: "He's going to be a business executive." (He became an advertising executive.)

My parents: "Go for it—who knows what he's going to be." (And I'm still working on it!)

Harvey's parents never showed, but being a rock 'n roll star wasn't in his cards.

The other Mark's parents were pretty old and voted to let Mark go whatever way he wanted. And guess what? He became a professional writer.

The irony of the story was—and this is exactly how I remember it—we were told the producer had the rights to the song "Sherry," which became a huge success for Frankie Valli and the Four Seasons around the same time line as the Stereos. For years, we thought fame eluded us by one small missed call by our over-protective Jewish parents. But truth be told, Bob Gaudio wrote and recorded that hit song for the Four Seasons. And, as we all know, it's still being performed as part of the brilliant production called

Jersey Boys, every night from Vegas to Broadway.

The Stereos still claim that they *almost* became a one-hit wonder.

GOOD-BYE, SECRET LOVE

Priceless! Me at 14 asking my secret love, Ellen, for a dance.

Ellen and I were such good friends that we actually made a pact to go to the high school prom together—as long as neither of us was dating someone else at the time. We made that pact in our junior year. But I changed the game when our senior year approached. It was one of those lemonade moments that define your life. So I'll take you back to a conversation I had with my parents in the summer of 1963.

"Mom, Dad, I've decided to go to the University of Maryland for college."

My parents were stunned. I think they were happy to know I really wasn't going to run off and join the circus—which I thought about a lot. It also became clear that they immediately saw dollar signs.

"Excuse me, what planet are you living on? Where do you think the money is coming from?"

"Never thought about it, Dad."

"Paul, looks like we need to have a discussion about the difference between out-of-state vs. in-state tuition costs." And so we did.

But then—and I honestly don't recall where this idea came from, my parents or me—but it was a doozy. We agreed that if I moved to Maryland in my senior year of high school and lived with my sister and brother-in-law, I would be establishing Maryland residence and then my dad would support me.

Wow! And the crazy part was all parties agreed—even my principal approved. I think the move was a brave thing to do, but I also think I liked all the attention. Even Ellen, as my friend and never-to-be-dated secret love, was really upset with the news. But I looked forward to the move. And when I look back on that decision, I thank God for the support I had from my sister and brother-in-law.

All in all, I was glad to have an opportunity to carve out my own new identity, even if it meant making new friends. Actually, making new friends was a big part of the excitement. So there's the lemonade!

JERSEY GANGSTER

High school in Maryland was cool because I was the new guy from New Jersey. In fact, they immediately thought I was a gangster. The bad guys in the school—The Turtles—actually tried to recruit me. It was so great to be feared and all because I talked like a Jersey kid, using words like *pawl*, *bawl*, *motha*, *fatha*. Ultimately, I wasn't a Turtle. I was more like a nice Jewish kid from New Jersey with an accent. But it did help create a perception for a while.

That, along with meeting my one and only non-Jewish girlfriend, made it a great year. Even though I had strict direction from my parents not to date a non-Jewish girl, I fell pretty hard for Pat. She was blonde, beautiful, smart, fun—and Catholic. So when I came home during my senior year, I asked my parents if I could bring Pat home with me to meet them. You can imagine their reaction.

"What? How can you even ask such a thing?" my dad said, shaking his head. "No, you cannot, will not and will never date a non-Jewish girl. Don't even think about bringing her here. And, by the way, if you disagree and ever consider getting serious with a non-Jewish girl, she will not be welcome here!"

Yes, my dad let his position be known. And my mom supported him without saying a word. I got the message, but that didn't mean I listened to their direction. It just meant I knew where they stood.

SPINNING TIRES IN AKRON

My girlfriend Pat was a great Maryland friend, but eventually it didn't work out. Nonetheless, I had fun at my new high school . . . that is, until the spring. That's when the news hit the fan.

In April of my senior year, I got a letter from the University of Maryland rejecting me as a state resident because my parents still lived in New Jersey. So that, according to them, was where I legally resided. I couldn't believe it. How could this be happening? I had moved to Maryland just so I could go to the university there.

I moved pretty quickly from placing blame—primarily targeted at my Maryland high school principal who should have known better—to accepting the outcome and starting on my lemonade recipe. The kindness of several of my New Jersey high school counselors got me into the University of Akron based on my soccer coach's recommendation.

But one really sweet sip of lemonade did come out of this new Plan B: My Teaneck friends had made it clear that from their high school yearbook to their senior class trip, I was to be part of the party, including going to their senior prom. Yep, I went with my best Teaneck girlfriend, Ellen. So we really did get to keep that pact we made a year earlier to go to the senior prom together—as long as neither of us was dating someone else at the time.

Funny thing about all of that? Neither Ellen nor I remember anything about that night . . . and we didn't drink, believe me. It was a blurred, but fun evening with a photo to prove we went together. And we used that same photo for our wedding invitation 32 years later!

After that, I headed back to Maryland, packed my clothes, kissed my sister, brother-in-law and one-year-old godson Ralph good-bye, then headed up to Akron. I spent one year in Akron—which I affectionately remember as the rubber capitol of the world and where spinning tires on a Saturday night was a big night out.

Sweet lemonade—Ellen & me at Teaneck's senior prom.

How's this for a lemon twist? Since I was pretty good at playing goalie in soccer, I got into the University of Maryland as an out-of-state sophomore and was awarded a partial scholarship for soccer. Needless to say, my dad was happy—and I was thrilled. My lifetime goal of going to the University of Maryland came true.

FOUR

Borrowing a Duck

Tried, yet true. Love the work you do, and do the work you love.
The money will follow, and the more passion you have, the more
successful you will be—in everything in life!

Going to the University of Maryland changed my life in many ways. I met my first wife Myrna through a mutual friend who said, "You should meet this Jersey girl I know—she talks just like you!"

Myrna and I played ping-pong together. No, really. She was quite athletic and tried to beat me. No matter what she says, she did not beat me in ping-pong.

But we did have a lot of fun all through our college years. She even was the source/blame (depending on how you look at it) for introducing me to my very dear and life friend, Ira Blumenthal. There are many Ira stories in my life—probably worthy of another book—but the best one happened when we were in a fraternity called TEP. We may not have been the best fraternity brothers, but we were pretty creative when it came to pranks.

The story all began when Ira and I wanted to borrow a duck from the University duck pond. I say *borrow* because we loved the ducks and would never harm them. We merely wanted to borrow a duck for the night. However, we needed one more person to serve as a lookout for our prank and enlisted the help of our fraternity pledge brother, Larry David. (Yep, *that* Larry David, who went on to become a great actor, writer, comedian, TV producer, co-creator of *Seinfeld* and creator of *Curb Your Enthusiasm*.)

So Larry, Ira and I went off to the duck pond and indeed did find the perfect duck. It was around 3 am. That's when we got the brilliant idea to go throughout our dorm and wake up all our fraternity brothers by knocking on their bedroom doors so they could meet the duck. We proceeded. The duck, on the other hand, went wild, running up and down the halls of the fraternity house and making duck doo-doo all over the place.

Pure Ira, pure joy! Laughing it up while wearing the matching pjs he bought us as a joke.

When the fraternity brothers stepped into the hallway, where it was dark and squishy . . . well, you can imagine what happened next. It was one of the messiest and funniest memories in my college life.

I look back at my years at the University of Maryland as fun, but I don't remember much about school, which tells you something. I fondly reflect on all those times, like meeting Myrna, which was a wonderful thing because we had many good years of marriage and produced two great kids. And then our kids produced my beautiful grandchildren.

Think of it, my decision to go to the University of Maryland led to our having a great extended family. And the lemonade doesn't get any sweeter than that.

I also had fun during my Maryland years playing soccer. That was largely in part due to my coach, Doyal Royal, leading my team to winning the ACC Conference Championship every year I was there. However, I was never more than the backup goalie. As much as I would like to say something heroic, that was absolutely the right place for me.

The starting goalie, Mario Janka Janka Janka something—I can't really remember the spelling of his last name—had become a first-team All-American and could probably play anywhere on the field better than the rest of the team. He was from Romania, could hardly speak English and had a mustache that made him look like a very old rock star. But I loved playing under Mario and was very grateful for the stuff soccer has given me. And that's why playing soccer has always been an important part of our family. So when I tell my grandkids to think soccer, it's in their DNA.

Perfect goalie form . . . before the game!

NO SISSY BRANCHES FOR ME

By the time I graduated from the university, I had been working full-time as a youth counselor at the Jewish Community Center of Greater Washington, DC. It was a job I loved and actually got paid to do.

I loved working with the kids, and I had a great boss, who wanted me to build a career in this field. I was heading in that direction and felt confident enough about my future. That same year, I married Myrna and we began an adult life together.

But everything changed—again—when the United States went to war with Vietnam. I graduated in January 1969 with a degree in one hand and a *report to duty* in the other. I was expected to join the US Army, which would lead me, potentially, to fight in Vietnam.

Although I was one of those people who believed in serving in the military and supporting our country, I didn't want to go to Vietnam. So I called the one person who actually knew what he was talking about regarding the army—my dad. He advised me to go immediately to the Army Reserve office and join the National Guard.

And so I visited the recruiting office, as did thousands of other guys. But there was a six-month waiting list to join the National Guard and even longer lines with all the military services except for one—the US Marines.

All the military recruiting offices were lined up next to each other. The cross-armed, recruiter-sergeant from the marines watched me going in and out of each of the other service offices, then motioned for me to come talk to him.

"There's no waiting list here, son. All you have to do is sign the line today, and you are a marine!"

I think I was stunned and said, "But, I just want the reserves—is that an option with you?"

"Absolutely! You will do six months in the reserves, then you're home, doing part-time duty, just like in those sissy branches . . . army, navy, air force. So come on down!"

I actually had to sign and take a physical, but it was obvious I was in. I went home and called my dad, whose reaction was something else.

"You did what? The marines? Are you nuts? You're Jewish! There are no Jewish marines. Forget Vietnam—the marines will kill you!"

"But Dad, it'll be fine. I'm in good shape. How bad can Parris Island be?" I said, adding a little lemonade to the mix.

Well, that proved another turning point in my life—I became a *leatherneck* who drank lemonade!

FIVE

A Jew, DI & Semper Fi

You will remember me!
—Sergeant Gunny Colley

Actually, I'm proud of becoming a marine and particularly proud of making it through my 10-week boot camp at Parris Island alive. Located in South Carolina, Parris Island was built on swamps across the river from Savannah. But believe me, this island with its stench of nearby chemical factories permeating the air was nothing like Paris.

Parris Island was a locked-down, inescapable, dismal island. And purposefully so. It guaranteed that US Marines in training—like me and 80 of my fellow boot-camp leathernecks who were naive when we pulled out of DC and landed in this surreal Marine Corps Depot—would have absolutely no distractions during our stay.

Now when I say that I made it out alive, I should clarify. I did have a couple of close calls, primarily because my drill instructor was one of those real-life, hardcore marine stereotypes you see in the movies. One story gives you the picture.

The drill instructor called us all together and told us to get ready . . . we were going to church in 10 minutes. Church? Did he say church?

I raised my hand. "Sir! Did you just say church? I am Jewish, Sir, and I don't go to church."

It was one of those things I learned not to do by my second week—don't raise my hand and don't say a word. But this was my first week and I didn't know any better.

"Jewish? Did you say, Jewish? What the hell you doing in the US Marines, son? I don't know what to tell you, but get the hell out of my sight and come back after you do whatever you need to do!"

He kicked me out of the barracks. His name was Gunny Colley, and he told me then, I would never forget him. And here it is over 40 years later, and I'm still talking about him.

I literally wandered around Parris Island and came across a young navy doctor who was smart enough to point me in the direction of the make-shift synagogue set up on base for the few Jewish marines who didn't want to go to church.

And there it was—a handful of guys wearing yarmulkes and being led in a service by a young rabbi from Savannah. It was like finding an oasis in the middle of the desert. I wanted it to last for hours. And I can promise you this: I have never, ever gone to religious services and prayed that it should go on and on. But, after a little while, it was over. Then we had a treat. The rabbi brought us bagels and lox with cream cheese. Wow, that was the best meal I had ever had!

Eventually, I found my way back to the barracks and settled in. A couple of pals asked me what happened, and I told them everything, including the part about the bagels and lox.

The following week when Sunday came and everyone lined up to go to church, the drill instructor looked at me and motioned for me to leave. Just then, one of the other marines raised his hand.

"Sir. I request to go with Bodner, Sir."

The drill instructor looked at him, then looked at me. "Martinez, what the hell are you talking about? You're not Jewish!"

And Martinez, who was from New Mexico and whose accent sounded just like Ricky Ricardo's, said, "Sir! I just found out my mother, she is Jewish. And that makes me Jewish. So, Sir, may I now go with Bodner?"

Everyone was silent. They all knew about the bagels and lox, and clearly this was a ploy. Finally, Gunny Colley walked over to him, told him to drop his pants. The sergeant looked down.

"Martinez, you're not Jewish, so get back in line—and prepare to go to church!"

For the next nine weeks, knowing there was a bagel with lox at the end of each week kept me going. I also did a lot of praying, but the bagels and lox were the real miracle. They were a wonderful reminder of how good it was to be Jewish, especially on Parris Island.

Six months later, I was out of the Marine Corps training programs and back home. I was in a transition period, which is the same as saying, I didn't have a clue. I was ready to become a husband and working man, but I really had more training as a marine than I did anything else.

IT'S A TOY WORLD AFTER ALL

Everyone had advice. It's amazing how much of an expert everyone becomes when you didn't ask. I was getting advice from aunts and uncles, my parents and my friends, but, stubbornly, I followed my own heart. The JCC offered me my job back, but I wanted to make it on my own, so I answered an ad for a salesman with Mattel Toys and got the job. I was there when Hot Wheels® was discovered. They were bigger than the electric train and amazing. Everyone wanted one, and I was having a ball selling them. But then an announcement came that changed everything—again.

My employer was having a contest. They just bought a company that made games and wanted to name a character to represent the company, something like a Ronald MacDonald® character. So I created one: Mr. Gamesman. And guess what? Mattel liked it. In fact, they liked it so much that they asked me to be the character and go around on children's TV shows, representing Mattel Toys. It was only for the Christmas season, but I loved it.

For four weeks, I played my funny-looking character, who loved kids and really loved playing games with them as well. I wore a funny, plaid outfit with a Mattel Toy sign on my shirt. The only other thing I had to wear was a wig. That's right, a wig that made me look like the Beatles.

One day, in Providence, Rhode Island, I was on a *Bozo Children's TV Show* playing the Mattel games with the kids. Bozo had one little boy on his lap while I was showing the boy how to play the games. And then it happened. With one swift hand movement, the little boy took one look at my wig and pulled on it. The wig came halfway down my face.

Bozo looked at me and cracked up—and couldn't stop laughing. They said it is still shown on TV in Rhode Island as one of their funniest moments in TV history.

It may not have been the Oscars® or even a local talent show, but I got the bug—the Hollywood bug.

SIX

Heading to Hollywood

Passion, purpose, ACTION!

Mattel liked what I did for them as Mr. Gamesman—but when Christmas season was over, they wanted me to go back to being a salesman. That was a problem. I had tasted the good life in TV and wanted more. So what else would a young couple struck with the acting bug do when push comes to shove? Pick up stakes. We chased my dream of being an actor and moved to Los Angeles, California. Myrna, me and our Afghan hound, Ari.

Ari was a significant part of our family. However, as much as we loved him, there was a challenge. We couldn't find any place to live that would allow such a big dog. He was so big that when he sat in the back seat of our Fiat convertible, it looked like there were three heads in the car. The one with the bigger ears—but equal in height to the other two—was Ari's.

One day, we were knocking on doors, trying to find an apartment to live in. A kind woman saw us, and since she had a dog of her own, she understood our dilemma. She invited us in, then called her landlord to see if he knew of any apartment openings. There was one available in Hollywood. He assured us it would be no problem to rent to us. We were so grateful for the woman's kindness that we wanted to meet her husband and catch up with them later for dinner. She called her husband at work while we were there to introduce us to him. His name was Lee Haber. I thought the name sounded familiar, but I didn't recall knowing anyone with that name—then it hit me.

It was one of those moments, which I now know as *bashert*—a Yiddish word used to describe something that isn't just a coincidence, but an event that is meant to be. Like destiny.

I reached into my wallet and found a crumpled piece of paper I had put there when my lifelong friend Elliot handed it to me before I left for California. Elliot had given me the name of one of his college friends who lived in Los Angeles and suggested I look him up because he and his wife were really nice people. The name of Elliot's college friend? Lee Haber! Amazing, but all true.

Lee and his wife Karen became our close friends. There are many stories about how Elliot positively affected my life, but none have more magic than this one.

ACTION, CUT, RELEASE

Our California life was an adventure focused on creativity. We knew every day was going to be something new and be completely up to us—we really had no plan. All the possibilities life could bring stood in front of us.

This possibility thinking attitude became a mental imprint for me. I approached every situation with an openness toward what good could come out of a situation, rather than not. However, in this Hollywood world I was attempting to live in, I soon learned that what I saw as a good growth opportunity, others saw as *their* opportunity to take advantage of others' weaknesses.

Take for instance an audition I went on—one of the many that was advertised as *open* (any sex, race, creed, color welcomed) and *looking for undiscovered talent*. I was sure this was the one.

The audition was held at a studio in West Hollywood. There were at least 50 people there, mostly in the young 20-something age group. The casting director had us all take seats in a large circle, then explained that he was looking for a couple of actors who would have lead roles in an Indie film. That meant my not needing to be part of any union to get the part. Plus, it was going to be a widely distributed film, so he led us to believe that we all should try really hard to do well in the audition. And so it began.

The director called on a young man and woman to come to the middle of the circle. They took their positions facing each other, then the director set up the scene.

"You are both deeply in love and haven't seen each other in over a year. The young man just returned from the war and walked into her home, seeing her for the first time in a long, long time. And the young woman has been anxiously waiting for him to arrive, spending the last year alone and loyal to him—not dating or even kissing anyone else."

And then . . .

"Action!"

Well, the two actors started to hold hands and say things sweetly to each other.

"Cut, cut!" the director yelled. "Be more in love . . . show me, don't tell me!"

He may have wanted these two strangers to act like deeply passionate lovers, but these actors were just two kids standing in front of 50 other kids. They didn't even know each other's names. So the young man tried acting the part again and again and again. Each time, the director made it clear he wanted more passion until he got frustrated with the young man and called me to take his place.

I was totally embarrassed. The most acting I had ever done was on the Bozo show as Mr. Gamesman. Now I'm being asked to kiss this actress and show this stranger that I was her long-lost war hero lover.

The first thing I did was ask questions because I needed to know more about the character.

"Can you please tell me where this character is from? North? South? Does he speak with an accent or a lisp? Was he injured in the war . . . or maybe he is blind and can't see her?"

Okay, okay, I did want to understand my character, but what I really wanted was o-u-t! Something didn't seem right. I asked the director where the camera was so I could do a better job, acting in the direction of the camera.

He pointed to the corner of the room. There it was—an entire camera crew filming the auditions. The light bulb went on. This wasn't an audition, but an opportunity for the director to get free acting on film and use it for whatever.

I stopped everything and turned to him. "Can you please give me a release?"

"A release?"

"Yes, a legal release for me to sign." And then he really understood.

"Get out! Get out of my studio!" He turned to the entire group and said, "If anyone else wants a release instead of acting in my movie, leave now."

One by one, the entire group started to stand up and leave the room. It was amazing! Not one person stayed there. We all went outside and exchanged names and numbers. We knew the audition had been a bad situation, so we promised to tell each other if we ever came across that kind of thing again.

The whole director-done-us-wrong thing didn't sour me from going on other auditions, but it shed some real light on the sharks swimming around those waters. I just made sure I didn't have any raw bait hanging around my resume as I moved on to fill my lemonade glass back up.

SEVEN

The Family Call

Our eyes are in the front of our heads so we can't look backward.

I was having a lot of fun, enjoying the craziness of living in Hollywood and so was Myrna. We became friends with some interesting people, including the Queen of 70s Pop, Helen Reddy. She had become very famous from singing "I am Woman" and was being asked to perform all over Los Angeles.

One day, when Helen and her husband Jeff were going to perform in a concert, they invited us to go along. We sat in the limo, where she put an 8-track into her tape deck—and got to listen to her sing in the car on the way to the concert. That was really cool.

Helen knew I was trying to break into the movies, so she did me a favor. She called the casting director at Universal Studios and got me a *blind audition*—one where you don't know where it's going to lead and there is no specific part you're reading for.

But I couldn't have cared less. It was my first big-time audition, and I loved just driving into the Universal Studios parking lot and having my name on the list.

The casting director was really nice, and after meeting me for a few minutes, he had me read for an animated film they were making at the time, *Charlotte's Web*. I auditioned for the part of Templeton (the rat) and created a funny, squeaky voice, which the casting director said he really liked. I went home encouraged by the audition and waited by the phone for my Hollywood-break call.

The next day, a call came in early in the morning—but not the one I was expecting. This phone call changed everything. My mother-in-law Jennie called from a hospital in North Carolina to tell us my wife's brother,

Philip, had been in a car accident.

I put Myrna on the phone, but she broke down. I held her, grabbed the phone, and listened. Philip had been driving home from work late that night and fell asleep in his car. He drove off the road and into a pole. He was killed. He was only 22 years old.

Philip had struggled with some difficulties growing up, but his life had just turned around for the better. His daughter Lisa was just born, and he and his wife Karen were just beginning their lives as a family. Now his life was gone. It was the first death in my life that touched me so deeply. I never again took life for granted—ever.

Real love . . . my first wife's mother, Jennie, with her husband, Mike.

Myrna and I packed our bags that day and headed back East to help Jennie bury her son. Leaving Los Angeles was a decision we made without hesitation—and with great love and concern for our family. It was the right thing to do.

So when the call from Universal Studios came in, I had to break the news that I had to leave town for a family matter. They couldn't have been kinder, leaving the opportunity for me to revisit them when I was ready.

And, sure, when Myrna and I left Hollywood, we were sad, but mostly we wanted to be close to her mom because we knew how difficult life was going to be for her. Knowing we would be closer to the family made us feel better.

Jennie and her husband Mike did the best they could to understand the tragedy and keep moving forward. In fact, they made a call on my behalf that led to my getting an interview and a job at WGHP-TV in High Point, NC. A real television station! And it was very close to where Jennie and Mike lived.

That year, we filled our lives with new friends and new adventures, giving me an opportunity to stretch my creative spirit. I was behind the scenes and in front of the camera, having fun and creating some whacky characters on a talk show called, *A New Look with Bill Boggs.* By the way, Bill and I stayed friends over the years, and he went on to some very successful TV shows in his career.

Myrna and I spent an important year with the family as part of the healing process. For us, the number one priority in life is being part of our family's hope for tomorrow.

THE UNDERWEAR SHIFT

And then, about a year later, I received another very strange phone call. It was an old friend from the Jewish Community Center (JCC) in Washington DC, who was offering me a job as the Youth Director of the new JCC they were building. Nice salary, benefits and they would pay for our move.

Perfect timing, I was ready to move out of TV and get into a more thoughtful career. Jennie and Mike were doing much better and were supportive of our move as well.

But the real reason why this call was so amazing was that Myrna was pregnant with Zack, our first child. We had been hoping and trying to get pregnant for a while—then one scientific lesson changed everything. My dear friends, Ira and his wife Arlene, also were trying to get pregnant, so we compared notes. It seems we were doing most things right—no details at this time, maybe later—but both Ira and I wore briefs. When we each decided to switch to boxers for more comfort, guess what? Our wives got pregnant almost immediately. Now, I won't swear that the brief-to-boxer switch was the reason, but it sure worked for Ira and me.

So from being sad one year earlier when we moved to North Carolina, we now had some sweet lemonade to look forward to as we moved yet again—this time to the suburbs of Washington, DC.

It only goes to show that when one door closes, another one opens, as long as you're looking for it. Live life expecting good things to happen, and many opportunities will open for you.

EIGHT

A Daddy's World

Believing in God is the beginning of inspiration—but believing God is living an inspired life.

Myrna and I were learning how to do everything right—including delivering the baby natural-style. What that really meant was Myrna didn't want any pain medication, so we learned a method where I helped coach her with specific breathing exercises.

When it came down to game time, Myrna was in the delivery room, screaming with pain and reminding me I was the cause of her pain. She doesn't remember that scenario too well, but believe me, I tried to calm her down doing everything possible.

I coached her very hard by doing the pant-pant-blow-blow method of breathing. Apparently I acted out that method a bit too hard because I started to hyperventilate. Myrna called for help. But when the doctors came rushing in, she pointed to me and said: "Not me! Him! He needs the help."

Well, they put a paper bag over my mouth to help with the breathing, while they wheeled Myrna down the hall to deliver baby Zack. There was no way I was going to miss this moment, so I put on my hospital gown and ran down the hall, breathing into the paper bag. When I walked into the labor and delivery room, I was there just in time to see the amazing miracle of life—the birth of my firstborn.

In this book, I write about the many reasons why I strongly believe in God. But there is no more tangible proof than when you witness the birth of your baby. I know we hear many different explanations of the creation of life, but from my experience and belief, there is no better proof of God than looking at your kids and their mother delivering a human life. That is all good, and the root word of good is God.

SHALOM, ZACK

Now there is a myth that my son Zack likes to spin. He tells people I left him—my firstborn—for Israel. The real story is a lot less dramatic.

I was working at the Jewish Community Center and was asked if I wanted to staff a trip to Israel, taking young people from the Washington, DC area along with teens from England. It was really an opportunity of a lifetime. Myrna and I discussed leaving Zack for the six-week trip with Grandma Jennie. We all agreed one-year-old Zack would be safe and happy—and would never remember us leaving him. So we decided to go. But it seems my son is the only living human being who actually remembers life at one year old. He must. He never missed a chance to remind me about 1974's summer of abandonment.

Still, I'm glad Myrna and I went. It was an incredible journey that began my love affair with the Jewish state. We toured the entire country, visited all the historic places, and met many of the country's leaders. But we also met other young people and their teachers, as we stayed at youth villages with housing. One newfound friend was an inspiration—and has remained so to this day.

We were staying at a youth village called Alonei Yitzchak, just outside of the beautiful seaside area of Netanya. A teacher named Itzhik Asher, who was also a sculptor, befriended me. One of the incredible differences between people born and raised in Israel vs. the US is their sense of appreciation of everyday life. Maybe it's because they have struggled with defending themselves every day of their existence. They just seem more genuine, direct.

It was clear from the start that Itzhik and I had many similar interests.

One day he offered to drive me to the coast and show me the home he was building. We drove motorbikes to the Mediterranean Sea and walked along the rocky coastline. There, amidst boulders that were centuries old, Itzhik was building his home—literally, brick by brick. He was the architect, landscaper and bricklayer. And he had made some beautiful art out of the scrap metal he was working with.

After an amazing few hours of seeing Israel through someone else's eyes, I had another surprise—Itzhik offered me one of his sculptures as a gift: a contemporary depiction of Moses holding the Ten Commandments.

My kids still think it's a praying mantis holding a matzah!

Remember, I said we drove to the seaside on a motorbike? Well, imagine carrying a two-foot statue wrapped in a blanket, while driving the crazy roads of Israel. My feet were flying as I juggled to keep my hand on the bike. The bike, sculpture and I made it back in one piece, thank goodness. And to this day, I have Itzhik's sculpture displayed prominently in my home. He is still in my life and is semi-retired after leading a prominent life as a sculpturer with exhibits worldwide.

I recently spoke to him and mentioned I still have the Moses sculpture he gave me.

"Paul, that is a one of a kind. It probably wasn't one of my best, but it is good to know it is with you and your family."

"It will always be in our family, reminding me of our friendship."

Truth is, my kids think it looks like a praying mantis holding up a piece of matzah. But I love it! It's a symbol of a deep connection with Itzik and Israel.

Myrna and I returned home, eager to tell everyone about our adventures—and, of course, renew our lives as doting parents of Zack. He was just over 13 months old then and had learned some new words: bye-bye. It's the one word he mostly remembers about our trip . . . and leaving him with his grandparents. But truly, it was a summer of life-changing experiences, which led to more trips to Israel as life unfolded.

HEADING BACK

After some years in the DC area, I was offered an opportunity to run the B'nai B'rith Youth Organization in Georgia and South Carolina. Another adventure—one where people say, "Shalom, y'all."

I like to tell the story about when we were living in Atlanta when my second son, Gabe, was born. Once when he was young, he came home from school counting.

"One, two, three, four, fiiiiiiive." He sounded like a true Southerner now—like a boy right out of *Driving Miss Daisy.*

"That's it. No son of mine is going to grow up with a Southern drawl!"

Of course, accent or not, we did stay in Atlanta long enough for Gabe to keep some of his accent—and now I think it's charming.

In truth, Atlanta was one of the best family experiences of my life. I remember noting how committed the families were to living in that town for many years, generation after generation. My friends there were having children who still had their grandparents living around the corner—and in some cases, great-grandparents. Something I missed.

It also was a town where I started to do my first professional writing. I always told lemonade stories, but one day I told a story that I later wrote and circulated. It went like this . . .

I was at work when I got a call from Myrna. She said it was important, so I listened.

"Zack just made his first *doo-doo* in the potty. You need to talk to him right now—it will help reinforce the good behavior."

So I did.

"Hey, Zacky, you made a *doo-doo* in the potty. I'm so proud of you! We'll have marshmallows after dinner tonight to celebrate." It was a lot cheaper back then to give your kid a prize. Video games weren't an option.

I sent that and a few other anecdotes to the *Atlanta Journal-Constitution*, who assigned an artist to my column and called it, "A Daddy's World." Years later, a wonderful woman by the name of Susan Davlin came to me and published all my articles into my first book.

All in all, we had six great years in Atlanta. To this day, we are still close friends with the folks who volunteered their time at B'nai B'rith to help out with the kids. It was the most fun job I had in my life! I now look back on it and wistfully use it as a lesson in life: The best combination in life is to do something you love to do—and get paid doing it.

But God had other plans for me, or least my dear friend Elliot did as well. This time, it was for a job working with Elliot in Los Angeles. Elliot knew I always wanted to move back to California. Maybe it was the weather or Hollywood. Either way, he offered me a job he knew I would love. And so, off Myrna and I went to sunny California, where my life changed again. But my goals were going to be different this time around.

MOVE OVER, MEATHEAD

Soon after moving back to SoCal, I quickly reunited with a close friend, Fred Rubin, who had left B'nai B'rith to move out West. Fred had landed an agent and began a long, successful writing career, working full-time in network TV and producing episodes for shows like *Night Court*, *Mama's Family*, *Step by Step* and *Archie Bunker's Place*, among many others.

The really great thing about Fred was that he never forgot his old friends. One day he called and suggested I audition for *Archie Bunker's Place*. It was the sequel to Carrol O'Conner's remarkable run as Archie

Bunker in *All in the Family*. Fred suggested a part in the episode called, "I Can Manage." Naturally, I jumped at the chance to have a one-week guest actor shot.

I took time off of work to experience one of the most memorable weeks of being up close and personal to the real deal. In the episode, my character (Mr. Langerman) competed with Archie for the affections of Teresa Forbes, a character played by none other than singer-actor Carol Lawrence.

You can imagine where that left me. However, the show became popular and I collected residuals for a while, allowing me to buy a piano with the money. A piano, I might add, that no one in the house ever played. But, oh, what a week it was. I had my own parking spot, my own dressing room and got to work with some of TV's greats.

However, I also realized that a Hollywood career was a marriage. You couldn't have it both ways. I chose to stay with my hospital career and fill my glass of lemonade with family and relationships vs. casting calls, which were better left to committed actors.

Nonetheless, I found ways to stay involved in the entertainment world here and there throughout my life. *Know your best lemonade formula and just keep sipping*, I say.

NINE

Just How Crazy Are Psychiatrists?

Crazy is all relative, which most of my relatives are!

California gave me an opportunity to learn a new business: the psychiatric hospital industry. A perfect job for a nut who made it on the outside . . . me.

I was hired to introduce our psychiatric hospital to the community, marketing our services to physicians and changing the negative impressions people had of the psych business. Admittedly, I was one of those who only knew what I saw in the movies. *One Flew over the Cuckoo's Nest* didn't leave a very good impression.

Well, this great story shows how much fun this job really was. The hospital had just finished refurbishing the gymnasium, which was a good opportunity to invite the public to the hospital for tours. Most folks haven't ever walked through the doors of a real psychiatric hospital. So I organized our staff into a basketball team and looked for a team to play against us. Actually the staff was pretty competitive, so they wanted to play a really good team. But I saw another story—one that included shining a light on a group of people who really had to deal with negative impressions and lives dealing with lemons.

I contacted the "Hollywood Shorties"—a basketball team made up of Hollywood's little people. It was a perfect event for us to attract the community. And it was good for the Hollywood Shorties, who could create a positive message about how they overcome their physical challenges. So we promoted the event and had a full gym of spectators ready to enjoy the game.

As we introduced the staff and the Shorties, we soon learned how competitive our opposition was, not wanting to give an inch. They played like the Harlem Globe Trotters with lots of tricks, including standing on each other's shoulders. And when we tried to call a foul, they made it perfectly clear that they could *never* foul—yet, we got calls on fouls. It became obvious early on. Our guys were not just going to get beat, but get beat badly.

The hospital staff took it in stride, but I had to live with the fact that we were the only team the Hollywood Shorties ever beat—and the news made it all the way to the *Hollywood Reporter*! Oh well, at least I made news in Hollywood. And the hospital became known as an excellent facility, so everyone won. It led to many more positive adventures and a career in healthcare that lasted through the rest of my professional life.

I worked with wonderful people, who also worked with crazy people. My job was to find psychiatrists who would treat our patients and make them better—a very difficult job. But I loved talking to the shrinks, and I had a lot of fun along the way.

THE WET PANTS INTRODUCTION

One of my favorite stories, which will make you fully understand why I had so much fun at this job, happened when I was traveling to meet a psychiatrist. Since I only talked to the docs on the phone before we hired them, I made it a point to meet them in person—back in the pre-Skype days.

I was waiting to meet this candidate, an unknown psychiatrist in a small town in California. We were to meet at a restaurant, but I had to use the restroom. I had a few minutes, did my business, and then used the sink to wash my hands. I had my glasses on, so when I leaned over to put my glasses down, I realized I had gotten my pants wet, right across the crotch! I took my pants off and waved them in front of the air blower to dry them. Just at that moment, someone walked into the restroom.

"I'm sorry!" he said, looking rather embarrassed. Before I could get a word out, he had turned around and left the restroom.

I dried my pants and walked back to the sink to get my glasses. Oooops! I did it again. I had leaned over to put my glasses on, but got my pants wet in the process. It wasn't as bad as the first time, so I took the garbage can, flipped it over and stood on top of it. I then turned on the blow dryer and waved the air toward my crotch, trying to quicken my pant-drying process. Just then, the same man walked back in and saw me standing there, this time on top of the garbage can.

"Oh, I thought you were finished. I didn't mean to interrupt you. So sorry."

And once again, before I could explain, he was out the door. I just had to laugh as I carefully bent over the sink and put my glasses on before going back to my table. Looking around the restaurant, I saw a man sitting at the table I had reserved. Guess who was sitting there? Yes, it was the same man who had walked in on me in the restroom. And it gets better since he was a psychiatrist. You can imagine the first thing he said to me when I walked over to him.

"Would you like to talk about it?" he thoughtfully said, but then he just laughed.

As a side note, this doc became a very good friend. And to this day, we will go out to dinner and enjoy an evening together . . . but he will never walk into a restroom with me. Now that's living with laughter.

TEN

Change—the Good, the Bad, the Painful

As bad as it gets, we need to get back up and keep going!

It seemed like all of a sudden, I turned around and the kids were all grown up. Zack had become a really accomplished soccer goalie, and Gabe had become a ranked tennis player. On the flip side, I had been traveling so much with my job that my wife and I hadn't realized that our marriage was no longer working. It was the saddest day of my life, having to tell my children that their parents were not going to stay together.

We had to move on, yes. But when the decision to split is made, nothing is more important than making sure your children know that your love for them will never change. And so we did.

Zack had been admitted into Yale, and Gabe and I moved to Beverly Hills. My dear friend Lucie Hinden was a teacher at Beverly Hills High School, so there would be a lot of support for him in his new environment. She took him under her wing and really was amazing, making sure his teachers were thoughtful and considerate.

Gabe became an excellent student, an elected leader in student council, and an elected captain in several sports. The move—although difficult—allowed him to become a successful young man. My divorce may be the most difficult lemon I had to handle in my life, but looking back at Gabe's personal growth, it also may be the sweetest lemonade he ever made.

Over the years, I remained good friends with Myrna. We knew we worked hard at being good parents to our children and made a commitment that our focus would never change. To this day, I believe our friendship has helped our children learn to trust again. But I wouldn't be honest if I also didn't warn against the terrible damage that divorce causes in a family. My hope for my grandkids is that they will have fun in their lives—

and when they are totally aware of who they are and what they want in life, fall in love and be the best partner they can be.

I've learned that marriage requires honest communication, genuine respect and a commitment to listen to each other, along with a heavy dose of always telling your spouse how much you love him/her. No one ever gets tired of hearing that.

WALKING RODEO DRIVE

I moved to Beverly Hills for Gabe to get a good education . . . really. But it didn't hurt that I loved walking to Nate 'n Al's Deli, off Rodeo Drive. I was the biggest stargazer in all of Los Angeles. I made sure I saw a star every time I went down Rodeo Drive—even if the person merely resembled someone famous, I would believe I saw the star. I must have seen Tom Selleck a million times. Of course, my friends hardly ever believed any of my Selleck sightings. But I did chat with Carl Reiner, Danny Thomas, and Don Rickles, along with many other stars, and had fun shaking their hands, especially when they were nice. I'd say Jay Leno was the nicest one. He was always kind when anyone came up to him. A genuinely nice person.

I won't mention the ones who weren't so nice, but they know who they are. It doesn't make sense to me. It is just easier to be nice.

I was working as the CEO of a psychiatric hospital, Gabe was doing well at Beverly Hills High School, Zack was sending back good reports from Yale. A pretty good time for all of us. Then it got even better.

Along comes New Year's Eve, 1992. My old Teaneck High School buddy, Ellen Levy Millstein, was there. Can you believe it? Right there at the same New Year's party I was at in Los Angeles.

We had renewed our friendship four years earlier at our 25th high school reunion. But, leading up to the reunion, I had thought Ellen had died—until my phone rang.

"Hi, this is Ellen Levy."

"That's not funny. We all know Ellen died."

Silence.

"Well, obviously someone got that piece of information wrong because I *am* Ellen Levy!"

After I picked myself up off the floor, she laughingly explained she did have some difficulties with her third pregnancy—apparently the word that got out was she didn't make it. But she did and was just fine.

And so we became pals again, like in the old high school days, and our families hung out together. While she had become a single person again, I was enjoying bachelor life in Beverly Hills . . . and then New Year's Eve happened.

The midnight hour arrived, the ball dropped and, yep, we smooched. And we liked it. In fact, we realized we liked each other a lot. So we started dating, then she moved in with me. The next thing you know, my company decided to move its headquarters out of Los Angeles to Vegas. Now that really changed things—again.

ELEVEN

Living Life, Vegas Style

The stripes you are born with can always be changed: they can either be demerits on a convict's sleeve, or achievements on a soldier's sleeve. It's up to you.

Believe it or not, in Las Vegas, lots of people live in regular homes, on regular streets, living regular lives. We found a nice suburban home and really liked living in the Entertainment Capital of the World. It surprised us, since neither of us gambled or liked it enough to do it very often.

I think in that way, I'm lucky because back in eighth grade, I lost $25 in about 25 minutes playing poker with my pals. Back then, that was a fortune. Needless to say, I lost the taste for gambling quickly.

Unfortunately, there are a lot of people in Las Vegas who never lost the taste when they should have. So there are many sad stories to hear, especially when you ride in the taxi cabs and listen to the if-only-I-had-walked-away stories of regret.

One particular cab driver almost got us into an accident as he kept looking at us in the back seat, wanting to tell us his story. I mean really, your eyes are in the front of your head for a reason—looking forward.

We liked going to the Strip, seeing the shows, eating at good restaurants, and just people watching. Vegas is also the wedding chapel of the world, which leads me to the next big change in my life . . . marrying Ellen.

I had been planning on popping the question to Ellen for a while, especially since she had asked me: "Where is our relationship ultimately going?"

That was a brilliant question, knowing full well that I thought it was going perfectly fine. There was no reason not to get married. In fact, the more I thought about it, the more I realized I wanted to get married again—specifically to Ellen.

And so I prepared to surprise her.

I meticulously planned a night to be remembered . . .
1. I decided to ask her on Valentine's Day.
2. I made arrangements at the Rio Hotel to go to their show, *Copa*.
3. I made arrangements with the chef to surprise her with her favorite dessert.

I could hardly wait. Then finally, Valentine's Day arrived. As we prepared to go out for the evening, Ellen had a headache. I would normally have been more empathetic, but c'mon. All my plans were in motion—and a headache was not in the plans.

I convinced her that the best remedy is to go out, enjoy the evening, and the headache would go away. Reluctantly, she agreed. When we arrived at the Rio, our table was center, first row, which really impressed Ellen. We ordered a bottle of wine, even though she couldn't drink due to her persistent headache. So, I drank for both of us.

Dinner was delicious, and then the dessert came. Drizzled in chocolate were the words, *Will you marry me?*

Ellen's first reaction was, "This dessert must be for someone else!"

But then the bandleader—as directed by me—stopped the show and asked what her answer was. Meanwhile, I was down on one knee, holding a beautiful diamond ring.

"Yes!" she said. The band, the chorus of dancing girls, and even the other patrons partied to our celebration. And voilà! Ellen's headache was gone.

It began the next chapter of our life together, continuing the relationship as best friends to now becoming life partners. And that is really another life lesson, I think: *It's best to like the person you marry as well as love that person because s/he will become your best friend.*

LESTER'S WHACKY HAIR SALON

Our lives in Vegas were primarily built around work. My company made me VP of Physician Recruitment, so I pretty well had a job that was all consuming. Being focused on work with only job colleagues as your pals isn't a good (or smart) idea. But for the moment, they were our only friends. And they were really nice people—most of them—and some were just hysterical! One of my favorite examples is a character I worked with in those days. Let's call him "Lester."

Lester was married multiple times and was a really fun loving guy. Everyone liked him. When he recommended a great hair salon—because back in those days, I actually still had hair—I agreed to accompany him to the barber.

We opened the door into the salon, and *yowza*—all the hairdressers were women and topless! Every single one of them. From the cashier to the women who shampooed your hair . . . topless, topless, topless. Only in Vegas.

Now if you're curious, they did a very bad haircut so I never did go back—really! But Lester did. In fact, he fell in love with the shampoo girl and may still be getting rinsed by her.

That's how we started to view Vegas. A bit weird, but a fun experience nonetheless. It really is a town where you can be whatever you want to be, but you have to be careful. If you raise your hand, you just might get called on. That's what happened when I became the founding President of the CineVegas Film Festival.

ME AND MY BIG MOUTH

We had finally started to branch out with friendships beyond the workplace. Seven of my friends were film nuts, like me. Big time. So we decided what this town really needed was a film festival. And who would be more perfect to voluntarily organize it? Me. The one with the biggest mouth.

I know by now you've read that I have done a lot of things, but a film festival? Really? What was I thinking? Well, it actually became one of the

Introducing Tony Curtis at CineVegas— he couldn't have been nicer.

highlights of my Vegas life, growing a grassroots organization with some very passionate people who believed in the mission and loved film.

We got lucky when Tony Curtis moved to Vegas, right around the time we were starting to organize the film festival. I cold-called him and asked him to accept our first Lifetime Achievement Award. He did.

Of course, we were a brand new film festival, but he took a chance on us. He was great to be around and loved talking to the community and his fans. I came to know him, but we asked Phyllis McGuire to do the honors of introducing him at the Festival. Phyllis, the great recording star, was set to introduce him at our awards ceremony, but she got carried away.

Charming as always, she went into a fun routine—then forgot to introduce Tony. She left the stage to applause, but that left me to do the only thing I could: walk out and wing it.

Here I was at CineVegas, introducing Wayne Newton as the new USO Chair.

A CineVegas highlight with Sidney & Bernie Pollack.

"The one, the only, Tony Curtis!" I barely got the words out. Introducing one of the great film legends and one of my personal heroes, now that was a moment I'll never forget.

CineVegas gained momentum. *The NY Times* called it, "USA's fastest-growing film festival." Sadly, several years later, when the economy really struggled, advertising and money started to dry up. That put CineVegas on hold . . . to this day. One day, it will come back—hopefully.

REAL WISE GUYS

I left the film festival business and went back to what I knew—the healthcare recruiting business. Ellen and I opened my own office. It became obvious that, as much as I loved being around her, working together was not a good prescription for our long-term health, or marriage. She was better off developing her own career, and I was better off with an assistant who was not my wife. It resulted in a much better, calmer, and happier home life for both of us.

The next few years were spent wandering in and out of the recruiting business and wondering if I made some career choices that were not too smart. I see past decisions as life choices that were meant to be and try very hard to have no regrets. But in order to write these stories with an open heart, I think that these years in Las Vegas were spent in a confused state of chasing misguided dreams. For example, my movie idea.

No sooner had I met an attorney friend who was helping me with a healthcare business transaction, when he introduced me to a real Vegas character. Let's call him Terry G., one of the original Vegas *boys*. I was fascinated by his stories, from scamming carnival games to creating the first private escort service. But underneath it all, I saw Terry as a character who really had a good heart—and meant well.

And so I got an idea to write a movie based on Terry's life. I raised the money, paid a professional writer to help me with the script and spent the next two years developing the project, which in Hollywood lingo is another word for dream scheme.

Terry and I met regularly to talk and get material for the script. It wasn't until I drove up his driveway to visit his home that a new reality hit me. There were bullet holes throughout the front of his house—all over his house. No window curtains or painted door frames, just lots and lots of bullet holes.

Matter-of-factly, Terry told me the story how the mob was upset with him and this was their way of communication. It seems that way, way back, Terry brought in a black-market version of the movie *Deep Throat* and rented a movie house to show the movie to the public. That also meant he went up against some wise guys—and they didn't approve.

At least, that was my way of understanding the story because I really didn't have a clue about his life. In fact, I tried to make lemonade from this experience and struggled. But I finally found one little way. Terry was just a guy who was getting older and looking for a friend who liked listening to his stories. And that would be me—as long as we did so in a public place.

We remained friends for many years, but lost touch as the idea for making the movie faded like the yellow edges of the now ancient script.

He did live his life fully and lived it on his terms. In my view, Terry was one of those Vegas characters who never allowed himself a chance to be who he really was inside. Just as the would-be movie title suggested—*Good Guy, Bad Guy*—he acted like a bad guy, but he always wanted to be a good guy.

Lesson? Better you should make up your mind and just be yourself.

TWELVE

Story of the Seagull

Live like a seagull, and every day will be complete.
—Dr. Alan P. Mintz

By now you have figured out that I was always into a new adventure, but professionally (or making money) never came from anything much except for healthcare.

And that led me to Dr. Alan P. Mintz, an amazing man and friend. Alan had a dream of creating a medical practice focused on healthy aging, where people could get help on how to become stronger as they got older, not weaker. I loved the idea, and he hired me to help build the practice.

I recruited their staff and their docs, then did some marketing as well as public relations. It was great fun. I finally was working with a team of people who loved living with a purpose. Alan and I would have long talks about life, love, passion and people. Once, he shared with me a story I would like to share with you. It's the story of a seagull.

Many years ago, when God was creating the world of people, plants and animals, there was only one creature that never seemed to listen—the seagull. All other creatures could be happy or sad, healthy or sick, but not the seagull.

Alan described in detail the absolutely perfect arrangement of how a seagull was constructed. It is the only creature known to man never to be sick—not one day in its life. Seagulls are born, they learn to fly, and then they soar every day for the rest of their lives . . . until they can soar no longer. And on that final day, they die.

The seagull inspired him.

"That's the way I hope we all live our lives—every day fully and completely. Then, when we can't live that way any longer, we die."

I've never forgotten that story. In fact, I try to live that same way to this day.

I was really happy working with Alan and his company during those years. But then, like the seagull, Alan could no longer "fly." He got very sick, very quickly, and soon died. It was so sad for so many of us who loved him very much. I knew it was Alan's way to say good-bye—not to prolong his time on this earth, but to move along. Or, as he used to say, making room for the young and the strong.

Alan had a big influence on me. He believed in my ideas and listened to my thoughts. He embodied the ABCs of great leadership: Appreciate, believe and commit to the people you care about, and they will inspire you to be greater than you ever thought you could be.

My focus on healthy living became part of my life. Ellen and I would eat smart, exercise regularly, and fill our lives with laughter. I continued to work in that healthy aging niche, and things were going very well.

We enjoyed seeing our grandchildren grow—and soon there were nine. Our extended family stretched from California to New Jersey.

Here we are today—one great big wonderful family! This is what life is all about.

Truly, there is nothing sweeter or more fun than getting together and having all of them under one roof. Our hope has been that the family would stay loving with each other and respect the differences in their last names, yet never forget their roots, as they too, will get pulled in many directions.

It's been said that you can't create a clear path for the future if you don't acknowledge lessons learned in your past. These next chapters pick up my life with the biggest lemon I've ever been challenged with—stage 4 non-smoker's lung cancer. My diagnosis on March 12, 2012, marked an entrance into my days of awe. My mind has never been clearer, and my taste for life never sweeter.

Time is moving on, but I'm enjoying each day with longer pauses. Nothing is taken for granted. And so I begin Act Two of my journey when life handed me cancer—and I found ways to keep making more lemonade.

ACT TWO

Oy, There Are New Lemons

THIRTEEN

L'Chaim—to Life!

When you're alone and it's funny, why not laugh?

Well, it was late March 2012, and there Ellen and I were at the MD Anderson Cancer Center in Houston. What a remarkable sea of people. The Center was packed with everything you could imagine a small city having—sans the need for a barber! On the other hand, babushkas are a hot item there. I'm thinking a fundraiser with the Jewish Federation logo embroidered on some babushkas just might be a good idea.

In true lemonade-life style, I made a few people laugh while talking about our loose slots in Vegas. I don't know why they thought my comments were funny, unless it was my Jersey accent when I said "slots."

I met with my oncologist, Dr. Faye Johnson, a kind and brilliant physician with a great sense of humor. She even looks like her picture on Google (unlike Wayne Newton and his Google picture!).

Dr. Johnson came out of the starting block with a surprise: All the tests taken in Vegas were good, clean images. Her team confirmed the diagnosis as lung cancer, so the only thing she needed was a unique test to further examine my biopsy tissue, looking for a specific mutation I may have. Come to think of it, that sounds like a Marvel Comics plot . . . the Bod meets the Hulk.

Although I had to wait a couple of weeks for my specific treatment plan, the good news was I could go home. She made it perfectly clear, there was nothing new or innovative in Houston that I could not get in Vegas. My doctor at home—Dr. Jim Sanchez, President of the Comprehensive Cancer Centers—would take the lead and keep Dr. Johnson in the loop.

However, before I left, I did learn the cancer had metastasized to my hipbone. Translation: stage 4 cancer. But to me, that only meant a stage and a number. Just ask anyone who knows me—they'll tell you how much I love the stage. So for this stage of my life story, it was time to dress for the performance . . . lacing up my boots and fighting like hell to win.

Why? Because I also love a challenge. I charged forward with a move-over attitude. Yep, Ellen and I were going home to rewrite the record books and create greater expectations.

So when we left Houston to go home to Vegas, there was nothing on our minds but lots of love, laughter and lemonade . . . and maybe a little vodka.

A few days later, I visited Dr. Sanchez for the first time and had a few laughs—really. Now, don't get the wrong idea. He is a gem. Brilliant, board certified in everything from canker sores to cancer. But he also proved to have a great sense of humor.

"Look, doc, I want you to know right out of the shoot. If you're thinking what I'm thinking—that this whole thing is a mistake—don't hesitate to give it to me straight. It's okay. I've gotten to know who my *real* friends are . . . mission accomplished! I may have to give back a couple of plants and free meals, but it's a price I'm willing to pay. *Nu?*"

Pregnant pause.

Finally, he cracked up laughing and said, "You're a *meshuganah!*"

He later admitted to being stuck on the word "nu"—Yiddish for "so?" or "well?" and often used after waiting forever for a person to respond. But his years working with Jews kicked in and eventually he got it.

I appreciated his upbeat style and clear academic explanation of the mutations that had to be analyzed and the treatment plan options ahead of me.

"So doc, what you're saying is, if I didn't have cancer, I would be in your locker as the picture of a healthy guy!"

Again, he crossed his legs to not pee when he laughed. Of course, I had to throw in that he and my wife Ellen had that laughter-pee syndrome in common, which got him laughing even more.

"Hey, doc, not to be too personal, but you might want to consider

Keep'em Dry panties—I hear you can buy them on the AARP site."

More laughter. He was a great audience, but also a great teacher. He told me the next phase of my cancer challenge was more scans (including a PET scan) to clarify where these pesky cells were living. He also suggested an MRI of my head.

"Of my head? Does that have anything to do with my humor?"

"Your humor," the doc said, "will do nothing but make you better, faster. But based on your jokes, I expect this MRI will show nothing."

Okay, he got me there. Now it was my turn to crack up.

I could see this was going to be a very special journey . . . with a great doc and my rock—my beautiful wife—beside me, not to mention my wonderful, whacky friends and family. Lots of lemonade to come!

IT'S VEGAS—THERE MUST BE A BETTER G-STRING HERE

By April 12, all the scans and tests came back—and so did a treatment plan: radiation. My radiation oncologist, Dr. Dan Curtis, introduced me to his staff. They were all terrific, but I really loved my nurses.

Anyway, I waltzed into the radiation treatment room, and there were my three nurses . . . all under 30. They helped me get oriented. I was good to go, sans jewelry and any other metal (fortunately, I passed on getting nose rings quite some time ago!). So they gave me the green light and said to put on my gown and get on the table, which I did.

Next, they explained the remarkable radiation therapy mapping, a very Star Wars-ish approach that would follow a pattern and directly zap my cancerous hip area. However, just to be safe, my nurses wanted to protect my private parts—and literally took a paper towel and draped it across the family jewels. Seriously, can you imagine? In this 21st century, next-generation medical world, I get a plain ole paper towel, not some fancy schmancy coverage.

Well, my marketing mind started to spin. And, based on a modicum of modesty, I have to say that I hit on a million-dollar idea. I'll share it with you, but if you bring it to market—I get my 5%.

Why not create a radiation-proof G-string? It could be called the *crotch bib*. Now if any of you marketing geniuses come up with another name, but it's for the same purpose, know that I already sent an unopened envelope to my home to trademark my idea. So I'll come after you!

Well, once the nurses realized what a brilliant idea I had, they all agreed to do testimonials.

Want to know a really funny thing about all of this? About a year prior to my cancer diagnosis, my friend called to ask if I could help him out. He was producing a commercial and needed an actor to play a doctor, so he asked me to send him my headshot. Problem was, the last time I had a headshot, I actually *had* hair. Oy, what aging lemons can do to a good Jewish boy.

Anyway, he took my most recent photo to the casting director and voilà—I got the part and had a ball doing the shoot. The commercial ran for six months and, as life's quirks go, it was for the Comprehensive Cancer Centers.

But it gets better. One day, well after I was diagnosed with cancer, Ellen and I were kicking back on the couch watching Sunday golf. What do you know, there it was—the commercial I did for the cancer center. And guess what? My oncologist was in that same commercial!

You can imagine my surprise when nurses started to recognize me. But the cancer center's administrator had a bigger surprise when I asked for a steep discount. Hey, professional privileges, right? We are still in discussions about that idea.

TOASTS

One night when we were having dinner with friends, the toast was very special. But when you think of it, toasts are always special. Glasses are lifted

90

at every life occasion—from a bris (I feel really bad for you if you remember your own circumcision) to weddings, birthdays, bar mitzvahs and even dinners that aren't necessarily milestones, but a different marker (like in the case of one good friend when he passed his kidney stone!).

Toasts are obviously about good health, your health, and just plain health. And frankly, that's how it should be. Now we've all been at events where the toasts were memorable, some unintentionally . . .

Like the toasted best man who toasted the young groom who married the older woman and spoke mixed-up words of Groucho Marx: "A man is only as old as the woman he feels."

Or the aging wife who lifted up her glass to her spouse on their 50th anniversary, only to say the words of James Thurber: "To my husband who has lived by his motto . . . Early to rise, and early to bed, makes a man healthy, wealthy and dead!"

And the snookered husband on the occasion of his and his beloved's first housewarming: "May our house always be too small to hold all of our friends."

Okay, okay. We all have our favorites, but the theme of my friend's special toast that night was the best: "L'chaim"—to life! From days of living with little to the days of living with abundance, "L'chaim" goes well on any occasion.

LITTLE THINGS

So there I was, on the fourth day of my radiation treatments, which had become my new morning ritual. I would arrive a few minutes before 10 to very personal and cheery "hellos" from everyone. The nurses kept me up on stories of their husbands, kids, and daily dramas. The treatment was mapped out and dialed in. Within 10 minutes, I was in and back out.

The good news was the therapy was definitely working—my hip pain had decreased.

My new routine made me realize how programmed we all get. Most of us find ourselves moving within a particular groove, pulled along by predictable schedules and a predictable way of doing things. I used to get up at 6 am without an alarm clock. Thirty minutes later, I was making coffee, followed by my usual egg-white breakfast and then out the door by 7 am on my way to Starbucks. That was it, every day, except golf days.

Wow, has that changed! Here's what I discovered. Sleeping in is boring—getting up at a routine time is a good thing. It motivates you to have energy for what you plan on doing.

So knowing the radiation treatment was at 10 am every day, I backed it up from there. Breakfast was a little faster, thanks to the radiation. I just touched the bread to make toast. Okay, maybe not. But actually, mornings became more easygoing. Ellen and I read the paper together while we ate our egg-white breakfasts. Yes, we still read the old-fashioned newspaper, not an online version—which to our kids is like having a TV with rabbit ears.

There is something to be said about slowing down, stopping to smell the roses. Just the other morning, I sat in the kitchen, looked out at our beautiful backyard view and saw an amazing red rose stretching its stem from my neighbor's yard. I got a peek at what may be the most beautiful rose I had ever seen, yet it had been growing there for some time.

Ellen pointed out that most roses take weeks to bloom, maybe longer. But I just saw it that day for the first time. Naturally, I hobbled out to smell the rose, then stopped in my tracks.

"What," I wondered, "if I wander into my new neighbor's yard, whom I've yet to meet, and she calls security or worse? Maybe she has a gun. Hey, cancer is one thing, but a bullet hole? That's really bad news!"

Just when I started to retreat to the safety of my nest, I heard a Kramer-like *helloooooo*. It was my new neighbor. I introduced myself and spent the next 30 minutes learning more about growing roses than you can imagine. And, yes, she did let me smell the rose, which had a beautiful fragrance, but made me sneeze for the next 15 minutes!

I tried all day to recall what that fragrance was. Later that night, I remembered: it was pure pink lemonade. You just never know where the day's little things will take you.

BRAIN TRAIN

Next up: Zapping the bad cells in my brain with Cyberknife®, a Star Wars procedure, sometimes called radiosurgery or stereotactic radiosurgery.

But a rose by any other name is still a rose. Its laser zaps the bad guy so we can move on. And that's a good thing because my brain MRI had revealed some small cancer growth. This highly progressive treatment would fix the problem. So, as a dear friend advised me, I chose to learn to love the knife!

She reminded me how our mindsets change when we choose to love—rather than fear—a procedure, a person, or an event in our lives. I had a few things to put on my Love List:

1. I love my new walking stick—I used to call it a cane, but now (remembering Bat Masterson) I see it as fashionable.
2. I love my morning glass of prune juice—no explanation needed.
3. I love driving to Starbucks—I recall my first day back being able to do that, and it was a beautiful thing.
4. I love walking in the pool—where I used to chuckle at the *old timers* who walked when I swam. This kind of exercise now gives me a chance to learn from my fellow walkers all about the early bird dinner specials.
5. And I love taking out the garbage—why? Because I can do it.

Love helped make this Cyberknife® experience successful. So may I suggest this? Make today a special day. Kiss the people you love, love the people you kiss . . . and enjoy the lemonade.

BIRD . . . OR BIRD BRAIN

Remember my story back in Act One, about Urban, my neighbor from Iceland who used to flip me the bird? Well, history has a way of repeating itself.

We've all been there—some driving mishap that results in a snap turn, beeping horn or slammed brakes, followed by an adrenalin rush of realizing either you or some stranger just avoided a calamity!

Fair enough. So here I am, feeling better than I have in a while and wanting to enjoy the 90-degree weather by taking a drive, meeting a friend for lunch, and putting the top down. As you probably can understand, I'm taking life much easier now, including my driving in the slow lane. It's called the slow lane, right? I mean the left lane is the *fast* lane, so the right lane must be the slower lane.

Anyway, there I was, following a line of trucks, RVs and little old ladies sitting on hemorrhoid pillows so they could see over their steering wheels. Eventually, I needed to pass a few cars and then, oops—I veer into the middle lane and hear a long horn blast. It clearly was no Jewish shofar blowing.

My unintended victim decided to hit her accelerator, pull up next to me, and then shoot the bird! If it weren't for the fact that she was at least 85 with a cigarette in one hand and a gnarly, bony fist holding her bird-like finger in the air with the other hand, it wouldn't have been so funny!

I started to crack up. That didn't help. She rolled down her window and literally pointed to the side of the road, as if she wanted to rumble. Thinking this might be taped for a reality show—AARP Does Road Rage—I reached down for my cane and held it up while gesturing, "I'm sorry . . . I'm a bit under the weather!"

Apparently, she assumed my cane was a weapon. She reached under her seat and pulled out a crow bar.

"No, no," I said, shaking my head trying to explain. I picked up my newly assigned handicapped sticker and put it up to the window to show her.

Then I mouthed the words, "I have cancer. It affects my driving."

At that point, she took both hands off the wheel and shot me two birds!

Well, I couldn't think of anything else, so I blew her a kiss. I mean, what else can I do? Love was in the air, right?

And guess what? It seemed to work. Maybe she hadn't been kissed in a car or anywhere else in a long time. She put her birds back in the cage, turned to me with a smile and, I swear, she mouthed the words, "Stay in the slow lane."

After that, I pulled into the restaurant to valet my car, meet my friend and enjoy a nice lunch. As I was leaving, guess whose car was behind mine?

I handed the valet an extra $5 and explained. "Tell the little old lady this is for an extra newspaper so she can use it in the bottom of her bird cage!"

I doubt she got the joke, but between the valet having a good story and my imagining her reaction, it gave me a great laugh and was totally worth it.

WHAT GOES 'ROUND

As I neared the end of my radiation program back in April 2012, I realized my daily regime would be changing . . . again. Change really is a good thing. Or, as it's been said, change is inevitable, but growth is optional.

My new friends at the clinic had become part of my life, interacting with them every day, kibitzing, and preparing my treatment. More is shared between friends as trust grows and that certainly was the case with them. We would talk about all kinds of things and laugh about the experiences I had gone through, from the first day of discovering the paper-towel drape to my then-obsession of counting out loud when the radiation beam goes on (just making sure they weren't doing their nails!).

One day, one of the nurses talked about her daughter not winning a big sporting event. Being only 12, the daughter felt her world had been shattered. With patience and wisdom, the nurse got her daughter to understand—perhaps believe—that she could get better by improving on what she did today. That may not be a profound lesson when you're an adult, but for a kid, it may be the best lesson ever learned.

Her daughter's reaction? "Mom, you're probably right, but you don't have to be right all the time!"

The point is, she realized her mom's wisdom and finally said, "I'll think about it."

So here I am, like that kid. I'm still thinking about life's lessons, learning through today's lessons—living in the moment with cancer. It's really about making up your mind to not just change, but grow.

I can't wait to tell Ellen about my commitment to grow. Well, maybe later, when we both get up from our naps.

A NAME ISN'T JUST A NAME

Today I received my first month's supply of Tarceva®—a daily pill that targets my specific cancer mutation—I called the pharmacy with questions. The druggist came to the phone.

"Hi, my name is Gene Poole. How can I help you?"

"Seriously, I'm not sure I heard you right. What is your name?"

Silence.

"Gene Poole . . . and I've heard them all before. So what can I do for you?"

I just couldn't let this go. "Mr. Poole, I grew up with a kid in my class named Pete Moss, but I can't imagine he went into the fertilizer business. And I had another friend, Jackie Bienstock, but she never climbed a beanpole. Mr. Poole, how did this happen? Please, there must be a story."

I took a few minutes to explain about my lemonade stories on my blog, and he seemed to relax.

"I went by Eugene most of my childhood, but in my high school chemistry class, the teacher actually put the name together and it stuck.

So by the time I decided to become a pharmacist, it just seemed to go with my DNA. Pardon the pun."

We talked about other great names and their jobs, and how sometimes a plan just comes together. He asked about my favorites.

"My Hebrew school principal, Seymour Herr. He was as bald as a cue ball! Then there were my three friends who were all named *Dick* and played poker with me years ago—Big Dick, Easy Dick and Little Dick. You can imagine who bluffed the most. And recently my friend, a kindergarten teacher, tried to figure out a new student's name on the class roster that was spelled *La-a*, whose phonetic pronunciation is *La-dash-a*."

Then he told me his favorite—a restaurant owned by Sam Minella and Ella Minella. The eatery is called *Sam & Ella's Restaurant.* No kidding.

We laughed at how parents don't really see the fuss when they name their kids, but how the kids have to live with the consequences—but he seemed fine to go by Gene Poole, and welcomed me to call back any time. He also was a great resource to use down the road, since Tarceva® became my lifeline for the next 18 months. Just by talking for a few minutes and breaking up his day with some fun stories, the daily lemons became a bit sweeter lemonade—it really is that easy.

FOURTEEN

Tales, Wine & Gestures

Laughter is the best medicine.
—Dr. Norman Cousins

Laughter is definitely an important part of healing—whether that's because of the endorphins or the good feelings released. Doesn't matter. The point is, I made a commitment from now on to do a whole lot more laughing. But I started to think, *what makes each of us laugh?* And when did we realize, hey, that guy is just a funny guy?

I remember being in junior high school sitting in the cafeteria and suddenly putting my glasses on my forehead, then sticking straws up my nose. It was funny to me, but as my friends laughed, it became even funnier.

Oh, how I loved those contagious giggles and belly laughs. Sometimes they were spontaneous, like the time when my friend and his dad were walking down the street with me. Out of nowhere, the wind picked up and oops—off blew his dad's toupee. Chasing it down the street to retrieve it… that was hysterical!

Back when my dad first got my voicemail, he would always leave me a message with the same greeting, "Hi, Paul. This is your dad." That would crack me up.

So there are naturally funny people and situations, but I also think we need to see the naturally funny in everyday moments. For instance, the other day while having lunch at a restaurant, I was walking back to my table after using the restroom. I stopped and turned around to head back to the restroom, realizing I had left my cane leaning over the stall door. Problem was, the stall was being used. I decided not to bother the tenant, but to gently lift the cane back over to my side of the door.

"Hello! Hey, what are you doing?" The voice from the other side asked.

"Oh, sorry to disturb you," I answered. "Just getting my cane."

"How do I know it's your cane?"

"Well, has anyone else come back to retrieve it?"

"No, you're the first."

"Then, I guess you'll have to trust me—it's my cane. Have a good day!"

I walked out and started to laugh . . . really, really laugh. I mean, that was funny. But what about him? Here he is in a stall and then sees a cane slowly disappear while he's sitting there, minding his own business. Well, I hope he laughed as well because he certainly made me have a better day.

WINE & DRUGS

In advance of my follow-up with my doc, I called the Tarceva® help line to ask if drinking a glass of wine at night would be a problem with the drugs I was taking.

"Is this something you normally do?" the nurse asked.

"No, but up to a couple of weeks ago, I normally didn't take a lung cancer drug either. So wine might be something I now would like to do. Would that be okay?"

"Are you thinking red or white?"

"Well, which do you suggest?"

"Actually, white has less acid, so it would have less of a tendency to react."

"That sounds good. But what should I look out for as a possible reaction?"

"Well, you might get a little dizzy, and then a headache and possibly some stomach issues."

"Hmm. That sounds like the same reaction I would get if I weren't on the drugs and drank too much!"

"That's interesting. How many glasses does it take for you to have that reaction?"

"Well, I'm a lightweight. In college they called me *O-B* for *One Beer*." So I'd say, probably three glasses of wine and I would have that reaction."

"Only three? My husband and I finish off a bottle most every night!"

"Really? And what's your reaction?"

"To what?"

"Um, to drinking a bottle of wine every night!"

"Oh, that would be too much wine for you to drink."

"No! I was talking about *your* drinking a bottle every night!"

"I don't drink a bottle every night."

"You just told me, you and your husband drink a bottle every night."

"Well, first of all, that's only half a bottle each. And this isn't about me—it's about you. So even half of a bottle is too much for you to be drinking."

"Well, so here we are, back to the beginning . . . still trying to figure out if wine is a problem with my drugs."

"I would recommend you wait to see the doctor, then ask him. And by the way, let's keep this discussion about my wine interests just between us, okay?"

"Sure, I won't mention it to the doc. But if he or someone else you know happens to read about it on my blog, well . . . it is what it is!"

"Oh, does anyone actually read your blog?"

"As of this morning, I've had over 6,000 hits on it."

"Yikes! And this story . . . are you going to write about it? "

"Sure, but not to worry. No names are ever mentioned. However, I would suggest one thing."

"What's that?"

"You might switch from wine to lemonade! Guaranteed, a better reaction."

TALE OF THE TAPE

My checkup in early summer was fairly standard. In my case, that meant having some side effects from the treatments and needing meds adjusted. And you know, just walking into the clinic would make me feel better—like the guy with no shoes can't complain after seeing the guy with no feet.

So I was ready for my typical meet-and-greets and getting weighed, except on that particular day, there was a traffic jam.

Sylvia, a 70-something, rather large women was wearing an A-line tent dress. Harry, a wisp of a man at 80-ish was clad in Bermuda shorts and high socks. And then, there was me . . . dapper as usual in my warm-ups.

Sylvia: "Let the youngster go first!"

Harry: "If it was the best looking, you would be referring to me, but based on age, I think that would be the kid!"

Me: "Really? I could ask each of you for your IDs, but I'll take your word for it!"

So I stepped up, got my height and weight done. The nurse made a note in the chart, then turned to Sylvia for her turn.

"Young man," Sylvia says to me, "You could've taken more time than that! Now I have to get weighed—and that is the most painful part of my treatment!"

She walked up to the scale, but didn't get on. She first had to go through quite a ritual:

1. Removed her shoes.
2. Removed her belt.
3. Removed everything out of her dress pockets, including a huge key ring, a bag of M&M's® and half of Walgreen's cosmetic department.

Then she leaned forward and spoke quietly to the nurse.

"Listen, you and only you can know this number—you hear? Do *not* repeat it. And under no circumstance, are you to say it out loud. Are we clear?"

The nurse smiled, as if she had heard it a million times before and then crossed her heart to swear silence.

Sylvia got on the scale, held her breath (as if that would keep the scales from tipping) and looked at the number. "You need to get this thing fixed! Maybe I'll bring my scale next week—it works much better!"

Now it was Harry's turn. Before he got on, he shot a glance at Sylvia. "Would you mind if I borrow a few of your things? Just the key ring and M&M's®—my doc wants me to gain an extra five pounds!"

She actually laughed. "Hey, why don't we stand on that stupid scale together and split the difference?"

Well, we all just cracked up. Now the nurse would have another good story to tell. We agreed to enjoy the weekend and see each other next week. Ah, the lemonade.

LET'S SETTLE THIS, SWEETIE

From diners to doctor's offices, at what point do we say, "No more"? One day while waiting for my Zometa® treatment—a monthly infusion to strengthen my bones—I could hardly believe my ears when the office clerk called out my name.

"Mr. Bodner, you're next, hon!"

I checked around if they were serving burgers and fries. Nope, just chemo and meds. The last time I was called *hon*, the server was wearing a pink dress, had a pencil in her hair and was chewing gum faster than Elsie the cow chewed her cud.

I walked into the infusion room, mumbling out loud. My IV therapy neighbor started laughing.

"Sweetie, I've been calling my customers *hon* for over 40 years. It's a sign of affection."

"And where were you working for these 40 years, may I ask?"

"Different places. Mostly local stores in my hometown, San Bernardino. Why?"

"Well, I always feel a little uncomfortable if someone calls me *hon* or *sweetie*. And I know it drives my wife nuts as well!"

"Is that right? What do you prefer to be called?"

"My name is always a good start, but sir or ma'am sounds more respectful."

"Sweetie, if I called you ma'am, I don't think you'd get much respect!"

"Not me—my wife would appreciate it."

"Well, when your wife shows up, I'll call you ma'am!"

"Listen, if I called you sweetie—there, I said it—sweetie. Doesn't that make you mad?"

"No, not at all. It actually sounds pretty sweet."

"But it's disrespectful calling a woman or man that. And *hon* is like out of a 1957 episode of *Our Miss Brooks*."

"Huh?"

"Okay, more to the point . . . should I say something to the clerk, whether in this office or anywhere else, if I feel uncomfortable with being called *hon*?"

"Sweetie, at this point, with you sitting here getting some juice in your veins to keep you going, I would take all the sweeties and hons you can—holding them close, letting the love pour in. There are a lot worse things to worry about these days than trying to change old habits, most of which are good intentioned to begin with."

I thought about that all through my treatment. When Ellen came to pick me up, the clerk turned to me and said, "Mr. Bodner, I hear your treatment went well today—and your numbers are looking good. See you in a month, hon!"

With that, I got it. I no longer cared what I was called as long as the message is a good one. What else could I say to the clerk but this?

"Thanks . . . and you, too, sweetie."

The clerk seemed to perk up with pride, but Ellen looked like she was about to take my head off.

"It's a long story, sweetheart. I'll explain it to you in the car!"

A WARM GESTURE

Sometimes, all it takes is a small gesture of kindness—one that probably went unnoticed by most, but said so much about the person's character. This was one of those moments.

When I was at the clinic in mid-June, I waited for a nurse to prepare the Zometa® IV. It was so cold in the facility that you could hear everyone's choppers chattering. I turned to my neighbor and asked, "Is it always this freezing?"

"You never get used to it, but you do learn to bring your own blanket. I wish I had another one, but I am afraid I don't."

I smiled and thanked her anyway. Then I turned to my wife Ellen and suggested she ask the head nurse about possibly raising the temperature. But Ellen remembered we had an "emergency blanket" in the car trunk, along with the "emergency" water, flares, and first aid kit. Perfect. Or, as I actually said with my teeth shaking, "Peerrrffeeeeect."

I find it amazing that as we get older and wiser, we put the most useful things in our car for just such emergencies. Believe me, just one look at our trunk, and you'll find an entire sporting goods store, a hat for every occasion, and stacks of sweaters all neatly packed in tightly zipped plastic bags.

Ellen came back with the emergency blanket in hand—one never before used. It was a souvenir blanket from a Jose Cuervo promotion at the Red Rock Casino and about as thick as a tissue paper. We both laughed.

Right about then, my infusion neighbor's husband came by.

"Sweetheart, would you see if they've made a blanket delivery today? My friend is a bit cold." (Note: She did not say *sweetie*.)

As her hubby went off on a blanket search, she turned to me. "If anyone can find some extra blankets, Norm can. He used to be in the salvage business."

Within what seemed like seconds, Norm was back, touting three thick, neatly stacked blankets still draped in their fresh laundry wrapping. He unfolded one and covered his wife, then unfolded another, draping it over my chattering bones.

"Anyone else need a blanket?" Norm shouted out.

A frail, elderly man—apparently without any family or friends there to keep him company during his chemo treatment—raised his hand weakly. "Sir, I sure could use one, if you don't mind."

Norm walked over to him, gently spread the blanket over the gentleman, then waited to make sure he was okay. "Are you more comfortable now? Need anything else?"

"Oh, thank you. This is heaven!"

We all looked at that sweet old man and started to laugh . . . none of us were ready to get *that* comfortable.

With our nods to Norm, we let him know his thoughtfulness was appreciated. His small gesture of kindness brought a smile of happiness to a stranger. Just another reminder that if you can find one way to brighten another's day, it goes a long way to bringing more lemonade to our lives.

FIFTEEN

Making Sense of the Senses

All you need is love.
—The Beatles

Everyone in our family knows you don't hang up the phone without saying, "Love you." But when you're initially diagnosed with lung cancer, it seems people you hardly know are saying it to you. The funny thing? You're saying it back.

One time, I was calling the security gate to leave the name of a friend who was visiting. The security guy says, "No problem, Mr. Bodner, have a great day."

"Thanks, have a great one, too. Love you!"

After an awkward silence, he had no other choice but to respond. "Love you, too."

We both laughed and agreed we would keep that one to ourselves.

BEING A WET ONE

Surprise—I found you! It never gets old when you hear from family, new friends, old friends, or even really old friends you knew over 40 years ago. I've loved every minute of it and learned how to keep a straight face, especially when they say, "Wow, you look really good, especially under the circumstances." Or, "Wow! You look really good—and how many grand kids did you say you have?"

It's true. Who talks like that? Not if you expect to not get a heavy eye roll, or at least a nod of being a bit nuts.

I realize most people lead with their hearts, so enjoying our oldness and doing the hair jokes never get stale. In fact, reminiscing with one another about yesterday's laughs is how we stay young.

However, I will admit to getting moist around the eyelids pretty regularly these days as I read some amazing notes from friends and family. I've been accused of getting sloppy watching Lassie reruns, but when I got a note from two brothers whom I coached when they were 10—and they now are 35 or so—saying they were thinking and praying for me, it pulled at my heart. All I could do is reach for the Kleenex® . . . or is it Kleenexes? What is the plural of Kleenex?

Some years ago, I learned there are only two types of people in the world. This is actually a quote from Carroll O'Connor, who was quoting Norman Lear. Back when I had my 15 minutes of fame acting on *Archie Bunker's Place*, I had a moment of panic, trying to remember my lines. Carroll O'Connor leaned over to me and said, "Remember, don't hold back. There are only two types of people in this world—dry ones and wet ones. The dry ones may be clever, but the wet ones live life with passion. So give me a wet one any day, any time, anywhere. And, Paul, you're a wet one!"

That's why I keep the laughs coming and the Kleenex® close.

THE NOSE KNOWS

One day I had to run in for a quick meeting at the doc's office. When his tech came in, my immediate impression was, "He's wearing my dad's cologne! Mennen After Shave."

Okay, referring to this lethal bottle of wood alcohol as a cologne may be a stretch. But for as long as I can remember, my dad would shave in the morning, take that big green bottle of Mennen, drop some in his hands, and then splash both hands against his face. Then I would hear a scream! The cologne would burn through to his pores and turn his cheeks blood red. But he loved the fresh feeling—and my mom loved the smell. Quite frankly, it was a fragrance I couldn't wait to smell. It meant all was normal to start our day.

Then later that night after the doc visit, my wife and I had dinner with friends, one of whom was a retired elementary school teacher. We laughed at some of our immediate associations with smells, which brought back good and not-so-good memories.

Our teacher friend had just bumped into an old student who is now an adult. He came up to her and gave her a hug, saying she still smelled just like second grade.

I recalled growing up with all the traditional ways to seduce our teeny bopper girlfriends—like when I bathed one night with Canoe so badly that my date's mom wouldn't let me in their house. Or the time I soaked my car seats in English Leather and still couldn't get past first base.

When my wife Ellen and I were dating, I learned she was attracted to a great cologne I was wearing. She swooned and asked what it was. I sort of made up a stretch and told her it was a personalized label, just for me. I used it for the last 10 years, then stopped. So here we were at dinner with friends discussing fragrances and she asks, "Why don't you use that any more? I always liked it."

Now I hear this? I mean, from Nordstrom's to Polo, I moved on. But, given all we've gone through with the cancer, I figured it was the least I could do. So on the way home we stopped at Walgreens. And, yes, tucked in the back counter, next to the nail files and deodorants sat one lonely bottle of my old *customized* brand—Jovan.

Of course, that got Ellen laughing hysterically. But know what? No sooner did I slap on that magic sauce than the memories of great days and fun nights started flooding back.

Whether it's to stop and smell the roses, or feel the warmth of a burning after shave, these are the days when you make every memory last—even if you need Jovan to get the egg off your face.

INSIGHTS VS. OUT-OF-SIGHTS

Insights occur every day. But, unless you're looking, those insights can become out-of-sights. Take for instance the waiting room at the CT Scan clinic.

I needed to have a procedure as a baseline before beginning drug treatments the following week. That is, five other strangers and I were waiting to be called for a procedure. The conversation began with one gregarious fellow asking an elderly lady how many more treatments she needed to have.

"Well, this was supposed to be the last, but I have to come back on Monday since the machine wasn't working yesterday and that delayed me a bit."

I just looked at her. She acted as if her vacuum broke so she is late cleaning her carpets.

"The machine broke?"

"In this desert heat, the fan sometimes goes off, so they have a delay. Usually, they fix it within minutes," another patient said. "So why didn't you stay?"

"Oh, I would have stayed," said the elderly woman, "but my ride needed to go."

"We would have taken you. You never have to worry about that again, seriously. One of us will always get you home."

And you know what? They meant it. As the tenuousness of life becomes incredibly real, people's kindness becomes even more important.

The elderly woman smiled. "I'll take you up on that. Besides, where else do I need to be?"

We all laughed and joked about the days when deadlines, meetings, and scheduled calls were a priority—and everything else went on the backburner, including quiet moments to reflect and listen . . . sometimes to strangers . . . sometimes to our inner voice reminding us to call a friend or view a sunset.

Reflection brings another journey. One that has had me quietly thinking as well as laughing aloud about how special each day is. It has made me aware of slowing things down. Of course, I've got a story for that.

I was driving home—sunny day, top down. I approached a four-way stop. All four of us drivers basically reached the stop sign at the same time.

However, with my newfound slow-no-go attitude, I casually waved on the first car. Off they went. Then there was the second car, who I also waved on. They hesitated for a few seconds, then inched their way on.

And then there was the third car—who waved me to go. But I thought, "What's the hurry?" So I waved them on as well. Well, the driver actually got out of his car, crossed the intersection and walked over to me.

"Are you okay? Nobody lets three cars go ahead of them in this town. I wanted to make sure you didn't have a heart attack!"

"No, no heart attack. Just not in a hurry."

He smiled. "Okay, but you better move along. You now have three cars behind you and they may not be so patient."

I looked back and waved. Then I took a deep breath and with a remember-the-Alamo yell, I shouted, "Slow down and enjoy the lemonade!"

ENTERTAINMENT IN THE GYM

I was feeling stronger and ready to go to the gym and pool, where all the regulars were hanging out. There was Bernie on the bike. His routine would start with 10 minutes of cleaning off the bike seat with a towel and Lysol®, then 10 minutes adjusting the pedals before he would set a blistering pace at one rotation a minute.

Then there was Sylvia, stretching. She asked Bernie for help so she didn't lose her balance when she folded her bones to touch her knees. Bernie, on the other hand, was reluctant to lose his rhythm, but gallantly agreed to help her. He had to kneel below her so she didn't fall down—I was sure he was going to propose.

Larry—the lifter—donned a cutoff sweatshirt that had tiny little moth holes in the back of the neck, where his enormous shoulder hair would peek through. He leaned over the bench press, adjusted the bar to the right height, and put five pounds on each side. Then the grunting began: *Upphh . . . upphh* 2 . . . *upphh* 3. The entire gym shushed him.

As entertaining as it all was, I was off to the pool. I finally had a breakthrough and was able to actually swim again. No more walking. The idea of simply putting goggles back on and gently moving my legs in a flutter kick was like climbing a mountain—getting high on endorphins.

Ellen watched me, enjoying my tiny triumph—that is, until I started singing the theme from *Rocky* after only two laps. She, along with the mahjong players who were sitting in pods around the pool, shushed me.

I didn't care. It felt awfully good to be shushed while I was relishing my victory and laughing at life's embarrassments . . . really sweet lemonade!

SIXTEEN

Bubbameisters

Say it often enough, and it must be true!
—Grandma Miller

I have shrinkage. There are very few times in my life where I would celebrate that. But in early July 2012, it was party time. I had received a call from my radiologist that the brain MRI done that week had shown reduced cancer nodules and no sign of new growth.

This was great news! My doc had said that "stable with no growth" would be about as good as we could expect. So when the radiologist called and said, "You have shrinkage," my wife and I cheered.

"Hooray! Shrinkage! Bring it on!"

It was pretty funny when he heard our reaction—especially when he heard my wife leading the cheer.

"The test result may have little or no real impact since your brain is the least-used muscle in your body."

"I resemble that remark," I laughed.

We knew we had hit a solid RBI. And even if we were in the early innings, we had earned a seventh-inning stretch. Okay, I've got baseball on the brain, so between shrinkage and curve balls, I'm going for the fences.

The other good news was I didn't need to dust off my mask for another Cyberknife® procedure. At least, not yet.

In Yiddish, like many other cultural traditions, there is an expression used when you don't want to bring on bad luck. According to the *bubbameister* (old belief), if you spit on the ground three times, you are avoiding the evil eye (*kein-ayin-hora*)—so we don't talk about it because we don't want it to happen.

That's another reason why Jewish people are so positive, from the earliest days of Moses. When he brought us the Ten Commandments, the

Jews were always saying things, like "*Kein-ayin-hora*, look at him carrying those big, heavy tablets—it's good that he never had back problems, but he should be careful and not trip wearing those sandals." Or this one: "*Kein-ayin-hora*, listen to what Moses wants us to do—now we have to wander the desert for 40 years, but at least we have some quality time with the family!"

My medical news may not have been quite worthy of biblical reference . . . but for a blessing going forward with any future scans, I'll be the first one to write an *Eleventh* Commandment: Thou Shalt Have Shrinkage!

A SNEEZE CAN MEAN SO MUCH MORE

One night when my wife and I were at the movies, I sneezed a few minutes after the movie started. Not such a big deal, right? Except that someone on the other side of the theatre yelled, "God bless you!"

"Thank you," I automatically shouted back.

Remarkable really. I was being blessed by someone sitting in a dark cinema who felt the need to do the sneeze blessing. We've all been there—maybe in an elevator, you sneezed. There was an uncomfortable silence until someone whispers, "God bless you."

Why we do that can be anything from believing in the legend that the sneeze blessing keeps the evil spirits away or that sneezing is an omen of good luck. But when you're the bless-ee, you realize how good it feels to get the blessing, regardless of the tradition's origin.

I must admit it becomes a conundrum when someone sneezes more than once—and most of us do. That same night after the movie, we went to a restaurant. A child at the next table started sneezing. I immediately reacted and said, "God bless you."

But the father held his hand up.

"Thanks, but he does 10 of these in a row, so best to wait until he's finished."

I laughed, counted the 10 sneezes and joined in on a communal "God bless you." It really felt good. Such a small act of kindness can sure make for a happier place to be.

THE LOOK

A lot has been written about the eye roll, cold stare, or raised eyebrow. So I'll just loop them together and call them, *the look*. Every guy knows *the look*, and every woman gives *the look*. But it's amazing how *the look* can reduce the strongest of men down to the weakest of sheep.

Case in point? My wife and I were leaving the doctor's office without saying a word. I waited and waited, then thought, "Wow, I'm going to get away with this one." The setup was perfect. I had received good reports and was feeling fine. In fact, I received an invitation by the CyberKnife® folks to do an interview for a Channel 3 report, which would be aired about two week later. I also had an invitation to speak locally about my *Making Lemons into Lemonade* series, which was to be aired the week of September 7. (I told them the lemonade was still being made, but I could speak about how to put the joy back into the *oy!*)

Well, as good as that week was, I developed soreness in my toes, which my wife Ellen insisted I get checked. Here's where *the look* comes in. She had to pick up a prescription at her doctor's office, so she called them, asking that I be seen when she comes by.

Reluctantly, I went, as a walk-in patient. It wasn't how I wanted to spend my Saturday. So there we sat, waiting and waiting . . . and waiting. I was growing more and more inpatient, grumbling how this was nothing more than a sore toe, how we were taking up space from some needy person who may be sick and dying. But no, they can't get in to see the doctor because I got there first.

"Mr. Bodner, the doctor will see you now."

So off to the examination room we went.

"Doc, it's just a sore toe . . . but we thought you should take a look, if you don't mind." The expression on Ellen's face when I said "we" was worthy of a thousand words—mostly unprintable.

"Well, it is a very low-grade infection and normally nothing to be concerned about. However, with your illness and taking Tarceva®, there is a frequent side effect of infections. So you were right to come in. I'll be glad to prescribe an antibiotic. I'm sure you'll be fine, but I do want to see you again in two weeks. It was a very smart idea to come by today."

Yikes! Perfect moment for Ellen to use *the look*. But, she didn't. We just thanked the doc for her time and walked out of the room. Still no look. Then we checked out, made an appointment for two weeks later. And still no look.

Whew, I felt like I was home free. And, as just about every married guy knows, sometimes it's better to keep your mouth zipped and wait. But I didn't do that. When we got into the car, I just had to say something.

"So I just want to say . . . thanks, you were right."

Those are the words that make marriages go on for centuries. It's never about the details—it's about always being right! And with that, she smiled, affectionately patted my knee and then, there it was. *The look.*

Ah, perfect timing. What else could we do? We laughed and drove off to the restaurant of her choice (my treat).

PUTTING THE JOY IN OY

I got a gold star at the doc's office. He reviewed the magic blood markers with me and noted one truly dramatic change: My cancer marker had gone from 18.0 (from when first diagnosed) to 0.06!

That was due to so many combinations of great medical care, great support, great love, and my family's belief in moving positively forward. But this was also about the spiritual connection. I'm finding it amazing how easy it is to do God talk with friends who are unhesitating about "praying for you"—and it does feel right. There is a higher power and when you ask for help and carry on a conversation, there are answers. That's why I take time to review my moments thoughtfully, placing them within a daily mix of appreciating every blessing. It deepens my belief system. At least it works for me.

I also credited my good news to juicing/diet changes as well as the visual imagery that sends me into the Zen zone. Put all that into the mixing bowl, tossed with the love of family and friends, and the outcome was hope rising.

With the good news, I took that go-get-'em attitude with me as I met a friend for lunch to celebrate. Also at that lunch was a new friend who was struggling with pancreatic cancer and had been reading my blog. She had been diagnosed in May with the stunning news. The cancer had progressed aggressively and quickly. She tried traditional chemo for a while, but "it was killing her."

When she decided that wasn't how she wanted to live every day, her docs told her to make arrangements with hospice, who are caring folks that would help in her last days. But there was no sadness in her clear blue eyes, no darkness in her soul. Quite the opposite. She had made up her mind that she couldn't control her death—death was part of life. And you know, even though her once shapely body was now thin from this disease, it didn't detract a bit from her still-beautiful face.

But it was her clarity that moved me. I've used that word before. When sitting with a friend who is deeply spiritual, words like "caring" and "kind" become passwords.

They laughed when I shared how I threw my gum into the trash before entering the restaurant—and missed—then leaned over, peeled the gross gum off the pavement and put it in the trash. Why bother? Because it was the right thing to do.

However, my new friend had a different experience entering the restaurant—slowly and weakly approaching the massive doors of the restaurant.

No one bothered to open the doors for her. Apparently, all the nice people had disappeared about then. I got angry and wanted to stand up and yell at all the patrons there, chastising them for not being "nice to people." But fearing some not-so-nice person would throw me out, I decided instead to keep my mouth shut, and then open the door for her when she left.

We agreed that appreciating every thoughtful gesture has become a signal of how people approach life—and perhaps, how their parents brought them up. You know, those niceties, like saying "thank you," or "you're welcome," or being a good listener.

At a time when the expression, "as long as you have your health," is taken for granted, meeting my lovely new friend put everything into a new and inspiring perspective. Listen, having to put up with my drug side effects is nothing less than a giant *oy*. But getting a gold star for my marked improvement changes that *oy* to sheer joy.

That all helps me remember how easy is it to open a door, smile when listening, and call a friend who just needs a little love. How easy it is to make everyday lemons into sweet lemonade!

GOLF IS A FOUR-LETTER WORD

By mid-September 2012, I was back out on the links. There I was one Saturday with my group of friends who have played together on a semi-regular basis for years. We're called, "the Jew Crew." As we've aged, the goal for birdies has become bogies—and the gimme putts have become "there are no gimmes in life!"

Even when we don't buy anything, we tip the cart girl for just coming by. I loved that I was out and playing, which was reinforced when I got tired and picked up on a couple of holes. My opponents philosophically commented that it was good to see me out playing . . . but I had just lost $5 for the last six holes!

That night, all the crew and our spouses had dinner together. This time, it was at our house—another first since AC (after cancer). So I was finding the conversation fun and getting super-charged with our golf story memories. The major controversy among us was who put chicken fat on their matzot when they were growing up. One of the crew who was New York born and bred said his family always ate the chicken fat as a delicious Jewish topping for their matzot. Well, I was appalled! I only recalled topping ours with jelly, butter, salt, and even peanut butter—but schmaltz? All you have to do is look at a jar of jellied gefilte fish and slowly remove those delicately shaped, wannabe fish to see what you have left. Imagine spreading that on anything! I think, if tested, it would have a sun protection factor of 500.

That said, we solved the world's problems that night without throwing any food—and we started the Yom Kippur holiday by apologizing for any wrong doings. Well, except for the names we called the guys playing golf in front of us. I mean really, playing that slow is a *shanda* (shame)!

But as far as I am concerned, playing at all is a gift I am thankful for. And it really doesn't matter what you play. Just have fun. Play with the kids, play in the park or take an adult play day. Remember to do it with love, lots of laughter and fill it with lemonade.

SEVENTEEN

Taking The High Road

Every day offers choices—we just have to make good ones!

"What's next?" my friend asked me. I had to stop a minute, realizing how many answers were possibilities. That could be about my life, wife, health, writing—or whether I'm on meds or not.

As it turned out, he wondered what I was looking forward to. Then we talked. With the excitement of what was soon to happen, our enthusiasm increased. For him, vacation was around the corner. He and his wife of over 50 years were visiting a place they had never been. Wow, just writing the number of years they've been together brings back the heart-warming voice of famed radio broadcaster Paul Harvey announcing names of couples across America—because there were so few—who celebrated decades together.

And we also had plenty to celebrate. The docs had given me the green light to travel, so our plans were to go to San Francisco over the weekend for the official naming of our newest grandchild, Orly. We've been blessed with nine grandchildren. Each child has become even more of a miracle. Yet another "clarity" that comes with cancer.

The idea of this upcoming fun trip and the happy days ahead absolutely changed my mindset. Of course, every day had its challenges. But in my new perspective, my bad day was better than others who had it worse. Managing my outlook was vital to how I viewed the future. I was committed to believing in the possibilities of life. So my planning "things to look forward to" was a good and much-needed step that made everything that much better.

WHY IS THE SKY BLUE

Once you're past six years old, that's not a question you frequently ask. But, as Ellen and I gazed at the sky, we did ask the question and noticed aloud how deeply blue it was. Did you ever think about this? Seeing the sky from a different perspective—squinting at the sun, running in the park, or walking in your neighborhood—doesn't change the color. It's still blue, maybe a shade or two different.

So every day now, we notice the sky and realize each time how it's a little different than the day prior. Think of this: For millions of years, the sky has never been exactly the same. There's something deeply special about that and our being able to get up each day and witness the uniqueness of that day's sky. That truly is a daily gift.

BE SAFE—DRIVE WITH ELLEN

When my niece Debbie was visiting us recently, we had a great time, laughing for two straight days. One discussion rolled around to life in the streets of Vegas vs. other places.

Now I love this city, enjoy the Strip and feel quite safe here. Debbie got the first two, but needed clarification on that last one. So here it is.

Back in 2011, Ellen and I went to a two-day weekend training program to learn about handguns, thanks to an invite from a dear, loving friend. A hardcore conservative. We learned much, did a lot of shooting and took some great photos—especially one with Ellen looking like a cute Jewish Annie Oakley.

Later on, I went shopping. And since guns weren't on our shopping list, we looked for some "personal security items." It seems the most dangerous weapon I could find was a Callaway 7 iron. I could do much more damage with that than a gun. I got pepper spray for Ellen that was disguised as a lipstick-ish container. She thanked me and put it in her purse.

One day we were driving along and I looked over at Ellen, who was beginning to clean her glasses. Problem was, she mistakenly took out the wrong container (at least, I think it was a mistake). She proceeded to spray her glasses, filling the car with a stench I could hardly mistake—pepper spray! Coughing, wheezing and unable to see, I pulled the car over. Oh, the tears from the laughing and crying. Well, we knew just how safe we would always be, knowing Ellen was fully armed.

Obviously the stuff works. At least we assume it works against the bad guys. Her glasses, on the other hand, were still dirty. So don't try this at home.

BLUE DENIM SHIRT

As 2012 was nearing its close, I had New Year's resolutions on the brain. I believe in them. After all, what do I have to lose? One of my resolutions for 2013 was to let go of the things you can't control and not get upset about the little things that may go astray. Like this . . .

Ellen and I had gone out to lunch. Later that evening while getting ready to go out, I couldn't find my favorite blue denim shirt. Hey, it happens. So we proceeded to back track.

"When was the last time I wore it?"

"Where was I when I wore it?"

"Where was the last time I saw it?"

"It's not like you can lose a shirt, unless you are wearing it over another shirt."

Aha! That was it. We both remembered I must have worn it earlier and taken it off when we were eating lunch outside at the restaurant. So, yeah, I must have left it there. I jumped in the car, headed to the place, but they were closed. Fortunately, the manager saw me and came out to help.

"I think I left my blue denim shirt here earlier today."

"Hmm. Nothing was turned in all day. But there was a homeless man walking around. He may have taken it with him."

Taking the high road, I smiled and said, "That's fine with me. If it helps him stay warm, glad I could help!"

I drove home, told Ellen the story, and we both felt warm and fuzzy. But the next morning, I really was missing that shirt. It was my favorite. So I called around and went online, but no store had that particular shirt in stock any more. I missed my shirt, then reminded myself it was helping someone stay warm. A good trade-off.

A very "shirt" story.

About a week later, Ellen came home with some items from the cleaners and said, "You need to see this!"

I go into the kitchen and there it was—my favorite shirt, fresh in a cleaners bag.

"How did this happen? Is this really my shirt? Maybe there was a mix up, and I got someone else's shirt?" So I called the cleaners to confirm.

It was clear. This was indeed my shirt, which had been there for at least a week. They apologized for missing it last time we picked up our stuff. After we had a good laugh, it hit us. What about the homeless man—not to mention all that positive karma?

The next day, I went back to the restaurant and casually left another shirt on an outside chair. However, the manager saw me, ran over with my shirt in his hand, helping me from leaving another shirt there. Well, it took some explanation, as you can imagine. Eventually, I convinced him to just leave the shirt there for whoever wanted it.

As I drove away, I saw the shirt just sitting on the back of the chair, sort of waving in the wind, waiting for its new owner. A week later I drove by—and it was still there.

But the manager told me something pretty interesting. "There's a homeless guy who comes by every evening, puts the shirt on, then in the morning, comes by and drops it off, placing it back on the chair."

"That's like continuing to pay it forward . . . or else he doesn't like the shirt that much!"

Either way, between our shirt loss and someone else's shirt gain, you never know where resolutions will take you.

EIGHTEEN

Pink Lemonade

There's a purpose to everything under Heaven . . . so when you're given any opportunity in life to celebrate, take it.

Have you ever had a chance encounter that led to your connecting with a long-lost relative or friend? There was a great movie playing on that theme back in 1993 called *Six Degrees of Separation*. Well, I think our family got down to just one degree in early 2013.

One of the first gestures of kindness we received after New Year's was from our neighbors who shared their amazing homemade tiramisu. That in and of itself wasn't so unusual. But as we talked, I realized they were telling stories that wound up being about my kids' lives!

"Wow," I thought. "How the world keeps getting smaller."

You see, not long before, when my youngest son Gabe was visiting, he saw my neighbor in the backyard and started chatting. In short order, Gabe learned that my neighbor was originally from Israel and later lived in San Francisco for over 30 years before moving to Vegas. Within a few minutes, Gabe called his wife to the backyard scene, then I joined the group. It turned out these neighbors were close friends of my daughter-in-law's Israeli family who lived in San Francisco. In fact, my neighbor had known both of my sons' wives since birth.

It was an emotional laugh fest with hugs all around, And, being Israeli, my daughter-in-law Tamara immediately got on the phone to call her family in San Francisco, creating yet another level of Jewish geography. Now we have more family in Israel and more future weddings to attend.

I share this anecdote because I love those "you wouldn't believe who I just saw!" stories. I think they're all amazing—and not just coincidences. They connect us on some basic level of history that creates a natural familiarity, which cuts through the surface stuff. Usually that's a good thing.

Sometimes old history needs to stay tucked away. Here's a case in point.

When I saw my high school friend in Vegas for the first time in 50 years, my initial and natural reaction was to greet him with a big "Hi, Ritchie!" Well, that took him by surprise. Apparently he hadn't been called Ritchie for many years . . . and now goes by "Richard."

No way. For me, he would always be Ritchie—but I'm not sure he agreed. And I sensed this wasn't going to be a reconnection that would last—as opposed to my reconnecting with my cousin, Carole. As a child, I only knew her as "Snooks." She may have been approaching 70, but she still smiled when I called her that.

Usually life puts you in front of these seemingly chance encounters for a reason. If you trust your instincts, you can turn them into another lasting lemonade relationship. And that, my friends, is what it's all about.

PINK GOLF BALLS MAKE PINK LEMONADE

Between Russian asteroids and Armstrong's steroids, everyday worries are easily forgotten. Seriously. Can you imagine going about your business, then some weird explosion occurs in the sky and *bam*! One thousand people get hurt. Now that helps you see life with new eyes, gathering up all that trivial stuff and filing it under "how is this a problem?"

That was my take by early 2013. I was feeling stronger every day and waiting for results of my scans. But as my docs would always say, "As long as you feel better, then the rest of the diagnostics will fall into place."

I did feel I could beat this thing. The science was working well—my blood work showed good, strong numbers. And, since taking Tarceva®, my side effects weren't using my body as a playground as much. So every day and every situation were cause for celebration.

Meanwhile my friends at the Caring Place (supported by another great organization, Nevada Childhood Cancer Foundation) continued to do amazing work, offering every service imaginable for every patient in the city—without mention of money.

Yep, my eyes were opened to the joy in life. And certainly, Ellen and I were blessed with lots of friends and family who shared their love with us. However, the humor in our daily life continued.

Living on a golf course seems to automatically create more stories than most—like yet another day when an errant golf ball found its way into our backyard. Three big construction-type guys walked around our yard, searching under plants with a mission to find their precious white golf ball. Let's face it, most golfers would rather retrieve their golf ball in quicksand than reach in their bag for a new one. So search they did.

My wife and I watched as they hunted intensely without any luck. Well, I watched as my wife readied to take her 9 iron and flail it against them. I held her back, pointing out that these guys—all wearing shorts in 45-degree temperatures so they must be from Buffalo—weren't going to give up looking for their golf ball, no matter how ferociously she threatened their lives. Instead, I would have to go out and defend her honor, and then they would probably feel more comfortable beating on me.

Well, we both laughed and watched them drive off. But within seconds, we noticed another ball on our lawn . . . a pink golf ball. Now most guy golfers don't hit pink balls. Just because. So we looked outside and sure enough, we see two carts with four ladies riding down the middle of the fairway with no concern for their lost ball.

We watched and waited, but they totally ignored the pink ball that sat in the middle of our yard in plain sight.

I turned to Ellen: "Isn't that strange—they couldn't care less that their pink ball is sitting in plain sight on our lawn!"

Just as I said that, I turned and Ellen was gone. She walked out to the backyard and picked up the pink golf ball, then yelled to the women, "Excuse me, here's your ball." Then she threw the ball to them.

"That's so nice! Thanks and come and join us next time—we have more pink balls, if you would like!"

I sat stunned.

"Why would you do that for the women and not for the men?"

"Oh, well . . . that's the first time a woman ever hit a ball on our yard, so I thought they would appreciate getting their ball back."

"Really? The first time? Now how would you know that?"

"Well, have we ever seen a pink golf ball in our garage bucket of balls?"

Mmm. Point well taken. Pour out some pink lemonade.

A WEEK OF GENEROSITY

Early in March, I experienced an unbelievable week with feelings of amazing generosity in my life. I received a round of hugs from my doc and his nursing staff for having even more shrinkage. We were on our way to being so small that you couldn't see the lung tumors, except for their "shell." That was a good thing.

My blood work and scans came back with one little nodule left in the brain—which for some smiling reason the doc said "no worries." The initial diagnoses a year prior showed 15 nodules in the lungs. But we were down to one. That's right, uno. So instead of knocking on wood or being worried about talking too soon about success, I celebrated.

What happened next was also an amazing act of kindness. Tarceva®—the drug that had been working so well for me—is a miracle for those of us who can tolerate it. But it costs a fortune, literally. The retail cost is about $6,000 per month. For most of us mere mortals, we need to get some fiscal relief in one form or another. And my relief had just arrived through the Patient Access Network (PAN).

Now I had heard of the CNN Network and ESPN Network, but never the PAN. Turns out they're focused on generously providing financial relief to people specifically who have life-threatening diseases and need highly expensive medication to keep them alive. PAN's donations are anonymous. So I can only say thank you the way I know best—telling each of you about their good work. You can find them online: www.PANFoundation.org.

I continue to be thankful for the kindness of old friends and new.

And because of that, my focus every day is about remembering to share the gratitude and pouring another glass of sweet lemonade.

NINETEEN

Lacing the Boots Up, Again

Cancer is a tough enemy, so you need to be tougher!

About two months after my shrinkage celebrations in early March 2013, I learned about a new tumor—one in the back of my pelvic bone. The good news was no surgery was needed. Instead, I would have another radiation procedure with the CyberKnife®.

Since I had undergone this procedure successfully back in mid-2012 on my brain tumors, I was confident it would work. And yet, sleep was difficult, which led me to *pillow therapy*. Why not?

I told Ellen that the Caring Place had brought in this new approach toward improving sleep—but I had no idea what it was. Debi, a physical therapist turned *pillow therapist*, analyzed my sleep position and recognized what was needed to align my body for better sleep mode: one pillow under my knees, one under each heel, one under each arm, one under each shoulder, and one large pillow between my knees. Count them—eight pillows.

The Caring Place has been a supporter of Debi's program and has a store to donate the pillows. So off I went home with the pillows, hardly able to drive.

That first night, I proceeded to take out each pillow and place it in its strategic position . . . then watched for Ellen's reaction. About 15 minutes later, after she stopped laughing, she asked if there was any room for her. Good question. I mean, I could hardly see over the mountain of pillows. But not to worry, we found a way to make room for Ellen.

Did it improve my sleep? Hmmmm—if I would stay in that one position all night—perhaps. Not my strong suit, I'm afraid. So somewhere in the middle of the night, I awoke to find all of them on the floor except the pillow under my head and one small pillow under my sore back. But I do think it helped. So even one weird lemon can be turned into sweeter lemonade—if you just keep trying and laugh a lot along the way.

FEW WORDS, MANY MEANINGS

Sometimes when a word has different meanings, it makes me laugh. Take the word "check up," for example. You can get a checkup at the doctor's office or you can check up on someone or even get a checkup if you're playing baseball. Well, in the fall of 2013, it was my medical checkup. And it was getting mixed reviews.

Sounds like a movie critic, right? Except the doc said there were new nodules that were in the back area, but treatable. There was good news, however. Most of the original nodules were g-o-n-e. Or in medical talk, resolved.

That's due to the excellent treatment plan I had been on. So instead of doing a total medical plan make-over, the doc suggested we rescan in a couple of months and make a determination then.

I liked the way things were going. Change means new focus, so this change meant we could set forth on a new healing program. But change requires an openness to it being positive—and that takes a certain perspective.

Like the other day when I went to Starbucks and the cashier said, "Here's your change."

"Keep the change," I told her.

"That's nice to hear for a change," she said.

"Well, when you're nice, people are nice. So maybe, there's a change in the air."

When I got home, I watched the ball game and heard the announcer say, "He got him out—with a change-up!"

Then my wife walked in and asked, "What are you wearing for dinner —are you going to change?"

I really don't want to change. I want things to be as they were. But life is about change. All we can we do is embrace it and make the best of it.

REMEMBER REAL VINYL

We were cleaning out the garage, when I came across an antique. A relic. An immediate swarm of memories overcame me. It was the great Paul Simon album: *Still Crazy After All These Years.*

It reminded me of The Record Store—a place in Teaneck that I mentioned earlier in the book, where my friends and I would meet and compete to get the newest albums that were just released. My thoughts drifted to our making plans to listen to a new record at a friend's house whose parents were going to be gone for a few hours, giving us time to invite the girls over to listen as well. Ah . . . and then Johnny Mathias would take over with his magic.

What memories of my favorite friend's basement. Black and white tiles, woody pine walls, and stairs going down to our own space. That is, until his kid sister would sneak down to listen and watch—not that there was anything to watch! We would just play the records, gently touching their edges to keep the vinyl clean so they wouldn't skip and ruin the mood.

As we turned on "Chances Are," the lights went dim and the familiar parental call from the floor above would be heard: "You kids all right? I don't hear anyone talking!"

It was a simpler time . . . and we had simpler truths. I remember mostly laughing at ourselves, even when we really messed up. Take for instance the time, a million years ago, when my friend's parents were leaving for the weekend. That meant one thing—party time. We invited 20 friends over to listen to music. Down went the lights as we danced cheek-to-cheek.

What was really great was the fireplace in his home. Ambiance, right? Well, we lit the fireplace and dimmed the lights further. Then we heard someone coughing, followed by the smell of soot filling the air. We quickly turned on the lights, saw each other and burst out laughing. It seems we forgot to completely open the fireplace flue, so there we all stood—faces covered with soot like a mask, except for our lips! It was hysterical. We spent the next 12 hours scrubbing the walls as we laughed and laughed.

Those were great memories. I believe it's the richness of memories that keep us happy. Those dusty albums or shoeboxes filled with photos. They're brimming with a lifetime of smiles, so never stop enjoying life's surprises today—then all your memories will be keepers.

WHEN MINI IS MIGHTY

Just when you think you've got this thing knocked out, here comes another curve ball. Ellen and I had just finished dinner at a restaurant with friends. We were about to leave to see a performance of *Wiesenthal*, when I suddenly lost hearing in my left ear. Having had that problem many times after swimming, I tried to stretch open my mouth and pop open the eardrum. No luck. I must have looked like a bobble head as I continued to open and shut my mouth over the course of a few minutes to no avail.

Then I started to feel dizzy—and my left arm and fingers went numb. Something was definitely wrong, but like anyone, my initial thought was denial. I excused myself to use the restroom. I watched the faces of Ellen and my friends, realizing they saw nothing unusual. I reached for my phone to call my dear friend and internist, Dr. Mike Jacobs. Still the old-fashioned doc that he is, I had his cell phone number to call any time, thankfully without the concierge franchise fee.

I explained what was going on. He calmly told me to go to the emergency room and he would follow up from there. When I walked back to Ellen, I quietly told her I wasn't feeling well and needed to leave.

After making apologies to our friends, Ellen drove me to Valley Hospital. Minutes later, they had done an EKG and a CT brain scan, ruling out a heart attack and a major bleed. I was relieved. But they also said more tests were needed—so I had to stay the night.

Several more tests later, both the ER doc and Dr. Jacobs agreed I had gone through a form of stroke, but even more tests were needed before a final diagnosis could be given. In the interim, the hearing loss and the numbness continued.

I remember feeling calm, thanks to the competency of the docs and nurses. By 12:30 am, I was in my room. They encouraged Ellen to go home and get some rest. Now as all of us know, a night in the hospital may cost the same as a Manhattan five-star suite—but it just ain't the same.

The humor at 3 am when they wake you for more tests is all in the way they say, "So, how are you feeeeeeelllllling?"

And I say: "How about you come back in four hours and I'll tell you."

I was stuck with many tubes for at least 12 hours, like an IV with saline solution. So when I was in the MRI lab and waiting for more tests to be done, I said I had to go to the restroom. The tech helped me as I pulled my IV on wheels, shuffling along the way.

Most guys my age will tell you (in strict confidence, of course!) that the strength of their stream is—how shall we say?—reduced with age. But the tech that night heard me going on and on and on and on . . . to the point where he called for a backup, thinking I had passed out and left the faucet running. But let me tell you, it felt so good. There had to be lemonade in there somewhere.

By Sunday at 1 pm, all my symptoms were gone. The docs diagnosed a TIA—transient ischemic attack, otherwise known as a mini-stroke. All my scans were perfectly normal, so the only prescription I left with was taking one baby aspirin a day. Apparently, the cancer had thickened my blood, hence the baby aspirin. Think of it. Tens of thousands of dollars spent in tests, yet a $3.99 bottle of baby aspirin would do the trick.

Listen, I'm grateful for the great hospital care received, great care at home, and great support from my friends and family. But I realized during that ordeal how unprepared we all are for such events. There I was feeling absolutely terrific one minute—and in a flash, I was pretty sick. Fortunately, I was able to fully recover. But if anything can leave you with a God wink, this was it. Because moments like these help you realize one simple fact: You're not in control.

What you and I can do is clear. Do the best we can and live every day with purpose and genuine joy.

IN SICKNESS & IN HEALTH

It's a well-worn phrase in wedding ceremonies, but when romantic love turns to soulful love, companionship is what matters the most. I lead off with this expression, since when we sign off on a lifetime of companionship, called marriage—we have no idea what that medical commitment will become.

In late 2013, soon after Thanksgiving, my doc had informed me that I had new tumor growth. He also reminded me that cancer is a very clever enemy, so I had to be tougher and smarter than it. The Tarceva® had run its course, but now chemo had to be considered as an option.

Thus another phase of my cancer treatment was about to begin. Ellen and I had our healthy breakfast, read the paper, and quietly enjoyed the warm November sunshine. There was an awareness that seemed sharper. Sights, sounds, and even colors were clearer. It may have been helped by my new contact lenses, or the post-turkey buzz was kicking in. But the reality was, I was about to begin chemo treatment, which has a way of sharpening your senses.

For those of you who enjoy the euphoria of the heady rush that follows a sweaty workout, you might be able to relate. But to feel that same clarity when you're about to flush your system with chemo seems a bit odd.

So the next morning, we watched the morning rush of patients filling the clinic's waiting room—mostly older folks who sat thoughtfully, waiting for their names to be called. Not a lot of chatter, but an acknowledging nod to newbies like me, from the *chemos* and the *chemas* who welcomed us to their club.

Some brought books or iPads®, a few crossword puzzles. Others just stared, lost in their own thoughts. The clinic seemed really busy, but always an atmosphere of kindness prevailed. Patients had an acceptance of their illness that I found astonishing, somewhat inspiring really. Each one moved forward with the treatment as if to say, "This is my new normal— just another day."

About fours hours into my treatment and only 30 minutes left, I felt good, strong and clear-headed. I had seen others get pretty sick. Two patients even got very sick with difficult reactions. So I felt blessed to be doing so well, yet fully aware that we must take one day at a time.

Naturally, I saw the humor in these everyday moments as well. Take the guy who was sitting next to me, seemingly waiting for his treatment to begin and falling asleep while reading the paper—only soon to be awakened by the nurse.

"What's your name?" As the nurse gently awakened him.

"What's your birth date?" she asked as she prepared to stick him with a needle.

The man abruptly sat up, fully awake. "I'm just here with my wife—not as a patient!"

Well, we all laughed when he realized he had been sitting in the wrong set of chairs. But, as he explained, "They're more comfortable, so why not?"

I had been watching all that from a comfy recliner in a clinic that allows for 10 rows of identical chairs, 5 in a row, with IV stands next to each. I thought, *Someone is going to come up with individualized lazy boy recliners, with built in screens, and make a fortune selling them to clinics!*

But not today. Instead, an image flashed before me. I was five years old, post tonsillectomy, and lying in a hospital bed in a children's ward. I remember it well for many reasons, including getting the post-surgery visit from my family and receiving the prize of a Howdy Doody puppet. It almost was worth the major sore throat I was feeling!

But I also remember the wonderful feeling of family being there throughout that illness . . . just like now. Caregivers—those sweet souls who accompany us patients on our journey—are the heroes. Some folks like me have their spouses, friends, or partners sitting to keep them company. Others have cousins, kids, or pals. No nicely wrapped gifts are necessary because just the very presence of these kind caretakers is the gift.

Sometimes we forget how much it means to say thank you to those accompanying us down these uncertain, lemony paths. So I'm reminded of the simple promise made in marriage because it exists in true friendship as well . . . in sickness and in health.

NEW YEAR'S DAY 2014

Kicking off a New Year means so many things to so many people. For me,

Bucket list item: Seeing a professional fight—so my boys and I celebrated Father's Day early in January 2014 to catch a boxing match at the MGM Grand.

it's always about taking time to list all the amazing blessings we have, our love and our friends, family, and support. It also is a time to enjoy the good feelings of gratitude and funny moments, like this one at the clinic.

As I listened to my music plugged into my iPad®, I needed to use the restroom. To keep things simple, I just unplugged the cord from the iPad, stuffed the hanging cord into my sweat pants, then held on to the chemo stand and shuffled off to the restroom. Handling all these chores is a funny sight to begin with, including navigating through the cracks and bumps in the aging floor. But after arriving at the men's room, I proceeded to drop trough, but then realized my headset cord was dangling dangerously close to the urinal. I immediately yanked all parts back to safety. Short of crashing the IV stand and almost grabbing the emergency cord, all I could do was laugh (yes, by myself) and look forward to telling all my chemo pals about my story. Sadly, they were all napping.

So I had to wait to share my latest tale. But that gave me more time to reach for my best lemon squeezer and find new reasons to smile.

TWENTY

The Butler Did It

Lemonade sipped slowly allows you to enjoy every long, sweet taste—so slow down and appreciate each day's gifts.

Today, as I look down the road, peer around the corners, squint to see the future, I realize there really isn't an ending to my lemonade stories—fortunately. I believe there are many more to come. As I stated in my introduction, the clock is ticking. So I want to bring some closure in this book regarding the medical and emotional roller coaster ride this has been for me.

So let's begin with the medical side of things. By mid-2014, I again was diagnosed with new tumor growth. This time, it was in the thoracic area, which led to a treatment plan that included radiation and the CyberKnife®. These medical conditions are fixable, yet carry some side effects, like back pain. I've learned to accept that each day brings its challenges, along with some emotional celebrations as well.

Emotionally, the theme of hope running through my life remains strong and forever present—in fact, it's more evident than ever. Take this incident, for example, that happened as I was wrapping up this book in early June 2014.

I was in Dr. Sanchez's office while he was ordering a CT Scan to figure out the issue behind the back pain. My cell phone rang just as the doc was walking out of the room to schedule the scan. That in and of itself was strange because I always turn my cell off for my medical appointments. Why it was turned on, I don't know—but I'm sure glad it was.

So who was calling me? My acting agent and friend, Barbara Lauren, who sometime earlier had me audition for the part of a bald butler in a commercial with Robin Leach. She called to say I got the part. What an adrenalin shot of lemonade! When she asked if I could do it, I knew that I could . . . or at least, realized that I could when I heard the words "Yes, absolutely" leave my lips.

The point is I *chose* to do the commercial, which is yet another example of my going full circle in this journey of turning lemons into lemonade. Sure, it's a small role with a couple of lines. But the idea that I could—despite the challenge of stage 4 cancer—participate in life in a way that I love (acting), should offer hope to anyone reading this.

If we can keep believing in the possibilities and the everyday blessings life creates, we can choose to live more positively, taking life's lemons and making them into a life filled with love, laughter, and lemonade.

So let's make this clear—there *is* more to come. And I'm looking forward to enjoying more adventures together!

A happy wife is a happy life!

Epilogue

Putting my affairs in order is done. We still have to go through our personal favorites to decide which child gets which piece of memorabilia. But this is our shtick, not theirs. It's not an act of gloom and doom. It is an act of love and legacy. Having my dad's US flag in my possession—folded from his funeral and sitting on my bookcase—is a daily reminder of him that I cherish. Having a teacup from my mom's special collection keeps her memory of elegance alive.

Accepting that part of life is also about accepting death is a great way to live each day. Not by reading the obituaries, but by reading that each person, great or small, lived as best they could. Some of us had more opportunities than others to make a difference, but we each made our own opportunities along the way.

But mostly, these final thoughts have to do with beginnings, not endings. Sadness comes into endings, when hope is not available. And this book, if nothing else, is all about hope. Having grandchildren is all about hope for the future as we teach them how to live their lives with passion and purpose, which in turn, gives them a sense of their future.

And knowing that we did our best every day of this life puts a smile on our face when we say, "We enjoyed the lemonade!"

ACKNOWLEDGMENTS

Writing these stories—and now telling these stories—has been my chicken soup for the last two years. But it takes many people to mix the broth, chop the ingredients, and make a really great bowl of chicken soup.

To my wife, Ellen, for all her support: I love you and thank you!

To my developmental editor, Ann Castro: Her spirit and talent are mixed into a wonderful combination that made this project happen and become so special.

To my friend and a mentor in every way, Gerard de Marigny: Thank you for your belief in me as a writer.

To my kids: You never waivered in your support and then reminded me of some additional wonderful stories that you will share with your kids.

My life friends, including Ira, Elliot, and David: You knew the truth behind the stories and still encouraged me to create this book.

To my sister, Sue, and her husband, Bernie: Their love and support still inspire me—as well as their over 50 years of marriage!

You inspire me every day. Thank you!

> *We all have lemons in our lives.*
> *It's up to us to squeeze them into lemonade.*
> *—Paul S. Bodner*

Across the country, Paul S. Bodner's presentations have inspired audiences to overcome adversity. Now, surviving non-smoker's lung cancer, his stories take on a new meaning.

Paul is the author of *The Lemonade Series*—a compilation of stories of how one person can positively impact your life—and *A Daddy's World*, a collection of witty anecdotes about everyday life. He is a prolific contributor to magazines and has been featured on TV and radio shows as a motivational and inspirational speaker. As a former TV and radio talk show host, Paul has met with success stories such as former President Ronald Reagan, Eli Weisel, Sidney Pollack, and other notables. The executive-focused *Modern Healthcare Magazine* recognized Paul as one of America's most influential motivational writers.

He served as a university instructor at the University of LaVerne, lecturing on the science of achievement, and often was commissioned as a keynote speaker for community organizations, corporations, and schools nationwide, inspiring educators with his book, *Teaching with Love, Laughter and Lemonade*.

Over the years, Paul served on numerous boards, including the Las Vegas American Israel Public Affairs Committee, the Jewish Federation of Las Vegas, and the Jewish Community Center of Las Vegas. Since his diagnosis in March 2012, he also has become a committed leader in the fight against lung cancer.

A tireless community activist, Paul and his forever-young wife, Ellen, live in Las Vegas. They have five children and nine grandchildren and enjoy loving life more each day.

Made in the USA
Charleston, SC
31 July 2014